CAREER DIARIES

OF A

VOCALIST

Thirty days behind the scenes with a professional.

GARDNER'S CAREER DIARIES™

NIKKI RICH

G G
C

GARTH GARDNER COMPANY

GGC publishing

Washington DC, USA · London, UK

Editorial inquiries concerning this book should be mailed to: The Editor, Garth Gardner Company, 5107 13th Street N.W., Washington DC 20011 or e-mailed to: info@ggcinc.com.http://www.gogardner.com

Copyright © 2008, GGC, Inc. All rights reserved.

No part of this book may be reproduced, stored in a retrieval system, or transmitted in any form or by any other means—electronic, mechanical, photocopying, recording, or otherwise —except for citations of data for scholarly or reference purposes, with full acknowledgment of title, edition and publisher, and written notification to GGC/Publishing prior to such use. GGC/Publishing is a department of Garth Gardner Company, Inc., and Gardner's Guide is a registered trademark of Garth Gardner Company, Inc.

ISBN-13: 978-1-58965-037-4

Library of Congress Cataloging-in-Publication Data

Rich, Nikki.
 Career diary of a vocalist : thirty days behind the scenes with a professional / Nikki Rich.
    p. cm. -- (Gardner's career diaries)

  ISBN-13: 978-1-58965-037-4

 1. Singing--Vocational guidance. 2. Rich, Nikki--Diaries. 3. Singers--United States--Diaries. I. Title.
 ML3795.R514 2007

  782.0023--dc22   2007050844

Printed in Canada

TABLE OF CONTENTS

		52 Day 10	109 Day 25
		56 Day 11	113 Day 26
		60 Day 12	118 Day 27
		64 Day 13	122 Day 28
5	Biography	68 Day 14	126 Day 29
6	Current Position & Responsibilities	71 Day 15	130 Day 30
8	Resumé	75 Day 16	134 Epilogue
13	Day 1	79 Day 17	
18	Day 2	83 Day 18	
22	Day 3	86 Day 19	
26	Day 4	90 Day 20	
31	Day 5	93 Day 21	
36	Day 6	97 Day 22	
40	Day 7	102 Day 23	
44	Day 8	106 Day 24	
48	Day 9		

ACKNOWLEDGMENTS

I'm lucky to have had a number of influential and supportive people in my life, and they all deserve my gratitude. Without all the years of unconditional love and support from my parents, George and Marilyn Rich, none of this would have been possible. They believed in my ability and nurtured me to develop it to its fullest. My late voice teacher, Ed Farran, was truly a living angel. Not only was he a wonderful teacher with whom I studied for eleven years, but he was also a great friend. My orchestra leader, Stuart Rosenberg, is responsible for introducing me to a roster of amazingly talented musicians as well as educating me on styles of music I would have never tried to sing on my own. The "Professors"—John Griffin, Brian Robery, Ken Truhlar and Rick Cinquemani—are owed my thanks for making our band such a real joy. John G. deserves special kudos for all his help with everything. Most of all, thanks to my husband, Glenn Earich, and our children, Hannah and Graham. They're the reason I do what I do—my inspiration and my sunshine. Their love and support is priceless.

BIOGRAPHY

My career began as a hobby, singing in musical theater and summer stock productions. Toward the end of college I fronted a rock-and-roll band and found my home as a vocalist. Over the years I've been a member of several bands, expanding my repertoire to include standards, ballads, swing tunes, R&B, Motown, Big Band and disco, plus material in Italian, Hebrew, Ladino and Yiddish, along with a variety of rock-n-roll tunes from classic to alternative. I'm currently the principal vocalist for Stuart Rosenberg's Music for Celebration as well as my band, Maryann & The Professors. I've toured with Stuart Rosenberg, Dr. Bop & the Headliners, and the Dark Star Orchestra. I've recorded a number of industrial and commercial projects including for Michelob Golden Draft, Bally's Total Fitness, Fisher Nuts, and the BBC. I've recorded and performed with Junior Wells, Barrett Deems (Louis Armstrong), Joe Walsh (Eagles), Frank Orrall (Poi Dog Pondering), Vince Welnick (Grateful Dead), Ralph Covert, Ben E. King, Three Dog Night, Paul Wertico, Howard Levy, The Bill Porter Orchestra, Joel Frankel, and Lynne Jordan. Beginning in 1995, for five seasons I sang the national anthem for the NBA's Chicago Bulls, and I similarly debuted with baseball's White Sox in 1999 and Cubs in 2001. In 2004 I became a co-producer of Singer Spotlight North Shore, a showcase for Chicago singers. In November 2004, my singing was part of an ad campaign in a *Wall Street Journal* article written about an ad for the Infiniti automobile.

CURRENT POSITION AND RESPONSIBILITIES

In my varying roles as a bandleader, principal vocalist, session singer, backup singer and showcase producer, a number of my duties overlap. As the leader of my own group—Maryann and The Professors—I'm in charge of just about everything. That includes a wide variety of marketing responsibilities such as writing promotional material, hiring photographers and artists to develop our promotional packages, collaborating with a designer to keep our Web site updated, and putting together the promo packages that are mailed out to prospective clients. I also maintain our e-mail address list, sending out notices electronically to promote upcoming public appearances. I coordinate schedules for rehearsals, conduct meetings with clients and agents to produce future bookings, select which material we'll perform, handle payroll, file tax returns, and organize performance schedules right down to confirming the load-in time, running a sound check, and making sure all the equipment ends up in the right place.

As the lead singer in my band, whenever we're performing in a public venue I speak to the audience between songs, telling them where our next appearance will be and giving out our Web site address. At a private affair, such as a wedding or birthday party, my duties are more extensive. I coordinate with the party planner or the caterer to schedule who will offer up toasts, when the wedding cake will be cut, and any special dance requests. I introduce the bridal party and keep the flow of the party moving. I need to read the room to see what kind of music will get the crowd on their feet. Once they're there, it's my responsibility to keep them there and have a packed dance floor.

As the principal vocalist for Stuart Rosenberg's group, Music for Celebration, my job is to learn any and all special requests, keep my book of charts updated and neatly maintained for the musicians to read, bring my own microphone and cable to each performance, show up on time, and be happy for the clients no matter what my mood.

Whenever I've been hired to sing songs for a songwriter, or to record a jingle for an advertising agency, my main directive is to get the track right on one of my first takes. Producers appreciate timeliness and great intonation. I listen to the track to learn it quickly and correctly, following whatever direction I'm given. I may also be asked to lay down backup tracks in harmony or in unison, again doing so on one of the early takes.

As producer of the showcase, Singer Spotlight North Shore™, I'm in charge of preparing the singers, confirming performance dates with the band, designing the program that lists the order of performance and the singers' biographies, confirming show times and dates with the club, leading the afternoon rehearsal, and hosting and performing in the showcase while also promoting upcoming productions.

RESUMÉ

LIVE PERFORMANCES

Ongoing
- Principal vocalist for Stuart Rosenberg's "Music for Celebration"
- Lead vocalist and leader of "Maryann and the Professors"
- Backup vocalist for "Dark Star Orchestra" on Jerry Garcia Band re-creations
- Leader and vocalist for the "Nikki Rich Quartet"
- Vocalist for "The Nikki and Fred Show" (piano-vocal duo)
- Substitute vocalist for the "Dennis Keith Orchestra/DK Rocks"
- Substitute vocalist for "The Bill Porter Big Band Orchestra"

Previous experience
- Session singer for BBC Radio 4 programs
- Substitute vocalist for "Phoenix," "Joey Hart Orchestra," the "Steve Edwards Orchestra," and the "Jeff James Orchestra"
- Substitute vocalist for the "Jeff Sandler Orchestra"
- Backup vocals for "Brother Brother"
- Backup and lead vocals for "Dr. Bop and the Headliners"
- Backup and lead vocals for "Slim Diggins"
- Vocalist for the "Peter Hix Orchestra" and the "Ron Bedal Orchestra"
- Vocalist for "Moon Zoo-Autopsy-Turvy"
- Vocalist for "The Earthmothers" (college band)

RECORDINGS
- "Music with Steve" – Steve Beno [independent label], 2007

- "I'm Leavin'" – Four Miles [independent label], 2007
- "Sermon to the Fishes" – Stephen Asma [independent label], 2007
- "Pure Vocals" Web site (assorted tracks), 2006 - present
- "Break Through Overground" – Nicholas Markos/Bee [Tie Records International], 2005
- "Row of Trees" – Jeff Lazaroff [Underground Records], 2003
- "How Long Has It Been" – Louis Yoelin [independent label], 2003
- "Songs for My Father" – Nikki Rich [independent label], 2003
- "Love Hurts Anyway" – Brad Mormino [Bred Records], 2001
- "Dr. Bop's Playhouse I and II" – Mike "Newt" Riegel [World's Most Beloved Only Child Records], 1998
- "Seven Stops" – Slim Diggins [independent label], 1997
- "Flourescent Pancakes" – Moon Zoo [Our Records], 1995
- "Funky Blues" – Frank Collier Band w/Junior Wells [King Records], 1994

JINGLES

National
- ATA (airline)
- Bally's Total Fitness
- Fisher Nut Company
- Heath
- M&M Mars
- McDonald's
- Michelob "Golden Draft"

Regional
- *Chicago Sun-Times*
- Green Bay Packers

- Illinois Lottery
- Midwest Express

Local
- D&L Dental
- Fuller's Car Wash
- James Automobiles
- Mobile-Tel
- Oaklawn Toyota
- Play It Again Sports

SHOWCASES & APPEARANCES

2004–present
Producer of "Singer Spotlight North Shore" and "Singer Spotlight Junior"

2002–present
Featured performer in "Singer Spotlight" showcases

1995–present
Featured performer in "Chick Singer" showcases

2007
National Anthem singer, Chicago White Sox (also 2001, 1999)

2001–2006
Featured performer in "The Local Vocal Brew" showcases

2004
Infiniti automobile feature for *Wall Street Journal*

2000–2003
Featured performer in "The Vocal Venue" showcases

2003
National Anthem singer, Chicago Cubs (also 2001)

2000–2001
National Anthem singer, Chicago Bulls (also 1995–1999)

MUSICAL THEATER
1999–2003
Soul Sisters by Joanne Koch
Midwest touring company
Role: "Sandra"
1988
The Wiz
University of Illinois at Champaign–Urbana
Role: "Addaperle"

1985
Joseph and the Amazing Technicolor Dreamcoat
Niles West High School, Skokie, Illinois
Role: "The Narrator"

1984
West Side Story
Theater 219, Skokie, Illinois
Role: "Rosalia"

1983
The Wiz
Niles West High School, Skokie, Illinois
Role: "Addaperle"

TRAINING
1991-2002
Ed Farran, voice teacher
Chicago, Illinois

1988-1989
William Warfield, voice teacher
University of Illinois at Champaign–Urbana

COVER SHOT OF THE LATEST MARYANN AND THE PROFESSORS DEMO CD.

Day 1 *JANUARY 16*

PREDICTIONS
- *Draw up a set list for gig with pianist*
- *Prepare promotional kits for mailing*
- *Discuss new Web site with designer*
- *Record track for an online music-for-hire site*

DIARY
This time of year is off-season for jobbing musicians. During the Midwest's winter months there are relatively few weddings, bar mitzvahs and fundraisers, perhaps because inclement weather poses a travel problem. I remember wanting my own wedding to take place in January or February because I knew none of my musician friends would have a conflict with the date. Thankfully I have several gigs

PAGES FROM THE LATEST
PROMO KIT FOR THE BAND.

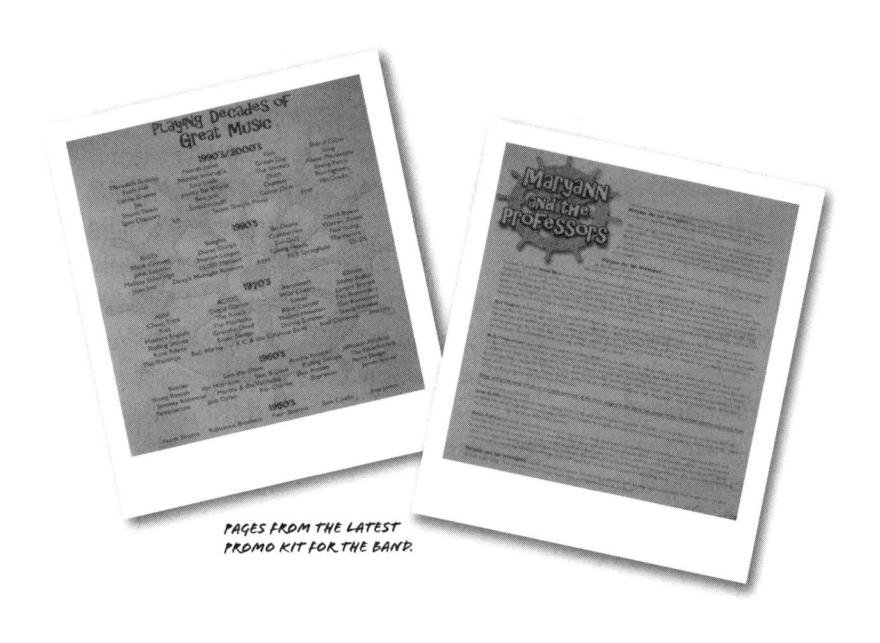

booked for the balance of this month, plus a couple already for February. My job today involves the first performance of a six-month run at a seniors' assisted-living center. This opportunity was posted online, and I sent the organizers a demo CD I'd produced that includes piano accompaniment. My pianist is an accomplished player with several original jazz albums to his credit. He's one of those musicians who are less than enthusiastic about playing weddings and bar mitzvahs. In fact, I don't know many jobbers who enjoy them, but you do what's necessary when you're supporting a family. Hardly anyone in this industry sets out to be a wedding performer, but if you get paid for what you love to do—making music—then it's a worthwhile effort. This particular engagement takes place one Thursday evening a month and runs for an hour, beginning at seven o'clock. I plan to build a set list that includes songs these seniors will enjoy, opening with "Sentimental Journey" and including material by the Gershwin brothers, Hoagy Carmichael, and Irving Berlin. The hour should go by quickly and will probably include from thirteen to fifteen songs.

I also need to assemble some promotional kits for my own band, Maryann and The Professors. I began with enough items to make up five hundred kits, of which close to a hundred have already been distributed to various agencies, country clubs, and other places where prospective clients lurk. The materials cost us close to $5000 to produce and include a number of photos of the group plus a sample CD. A full-color broadsheet shows the band in casual attire, sitting aboard a mockup of the boat S.S. Minnow—the name of the group and everything associated with it stems from the old television show, *Gilligan's Island*—plus there's a black-and-white sheet with the five of us dressed in formal clothes. The remainder of the kit, printed on heavy stock that's very shiny, includes biographies of everyone in the group plus a list of past clients, testimonials from several among them, and a list of songs we perform. The enclosed CD has a full-color insert and a group picture printed directly on the CD's face. The kit also contains a refrigerator magnet with our logo on it. The mailing envelope is sealed with a logo-inspired sticker, and our return address label has the band's name on it along with cartoon caricatures of each band member's face. After preparing several kits for mailing

THE "TESTIMONIALS" PAGE OF THE PROMO KIT.

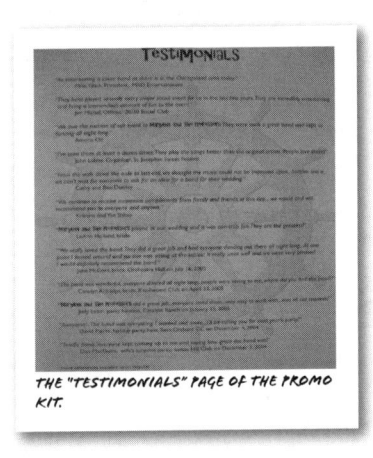

I send an e-mail inquiry to our Web designer, seeking an update on the new site he's building for us. After dropping the kits into a corner mailbox I'm off to our lead guitar player's house. He has his own studio where he records bands and quite a few voiceovers.

I'm listed on a Web site that serves as a source for singers, producers, arrangers, and lyricists for fledging songwriters who require assistance. Writers need singers to perform their songs so they can be peddled to record labels, where they hope to sell their songs to an established artist. Other people are looking for publishing deals or are entering songwriting contests. It's not a great deal of money, but the work is fairly simple. The Web site supplies me with two tracks, one with the vocal line sampled on it and one without. I e-mail the non-sampled track to my studio guy so we can record directly onto it. Once it's finished we send the track to the company, which then forwards it to the client. About ten days later a payment shows up in my PayPal account. I also post a regular ad on Craig's List that offers a similar service. The responses I receive from that posting earn me a bit more money, since it cuts out the middleman.

LESSONS/PROBLEMS

Doing an effective job of marketing, whether as a solo act or as part of a group, is just as important as performing well. A slick promo pack goes a long way to capturing the attention you need, and having a great band along with the fancy kit only enhances the overall package. It took many years in this business before I understood that. The idea of a huge marketing outlay, with no guarantee of recouping it, was an overwhelming concept. I figured that the band is good and the demo sounds pretty good, and that should be enough. The answer to that is, you still need to invest in marketing. I was hesitant to redo our Web site, but the old one is pretty plain and the thought of people going to it after seeing our new promo kits was depressing. Our next marketing project will involve the production of a DVD, but that will have to wait.

MY FIRST CHICAGO BULLS ANTHEM AT THE OLD CHICAGO STADIUM. BULLS VS. ORLANDO MAGIC.

Day 2 JANUARY 17

PREDICTIONS
- Ship out more band promo kits
- Re-record the national anthem for submission to a baseball team

DIARY
Today I'm sending out a promo kit to a woman who was referred to our band by the events manager at a local country club. She and her husband are planning a bat mitzvah party for her daughter there in October. Bar- and bat mitzvahs can prove tricky, since the audience is made up of prepubescent, anxiety-ridden 12- and 13-year-olds. These parties typically book DJs and an entourage that includes an experienced emcee plus four or five high school-age

guys and gals to corral the kids, teach them dance steps, and run contests complete with prizes. A live band is more of a novelty for this crowd. Since the event manager at this club was happy with a bar mitzvah we'd played there last November, I sent her a promo package for her file. Upon receiving a call from this prospective client, I was thrilled to hear that the country club had recommended us.

I also play quite a few of these celebrations with my regular jobbing orchestra. For those gigs, my duties include much more than just singing. In order to keep the cost to the client down, the orchestra leader may tell them there's no need to spend extra on a party organizer. The orchestra singer is then tasked with rounding up the kids, running the contests, and handing out prizes. There are times when the parents forget to stock up on prizes for the dance contests, and I've found myself running down to the nearest store to pick up a dozen super-large candy bars. I always expect to be paid extra for this type of work. After all, I'm a professional singer, not a camp counselor.

Once I write a cover letter and assemble the elements of a kit, I contact some booking agencies via e-mail to see if they're looking to add a new band to their roster. When I call to find out the name of the person to whom the kit should be addressed, I'm pleased to hear that several of the agents actually know our band and are willing to review our material. We may never get any bookings from some of them, but it can't hurt to pass out as many marketing items as possible. In the Chicago area there are dozens of agencies

AN OUTDOOR SUMMER CONCERT.

like these, ranging from small one- or two-person operations to major full-service offices. It's my intention to locate as many of them as possible and make sure each one has our demo CD and promo material on hand. I picked up a comprehensive list of agencies from a trade show I attended last November. This particular exhibition is run by the Illinois Park District Association and is designed specifically for park districts around the state to gather information on available entertainment for their summer concert series.

I mail the promo to the prospective bat mitzvah client, and then I'm off to our lead guitarist's house to do some recording. The Chicago Cubs organization has asked me to re-submit a copy of my singing of the national anthem. I've performed there in two previous seasons, but it's their requirement to receive a new submission every year. The version I've been using is about ten years old and is stored on a cassette. It seems like a good idea to redo it and burn it to a CD.

LESSONS/PROBLEMS
Being flexible and having the willingness to perform duties beyond music increases a singer's value, both to the bandleader and to the client. Acting as the emcee for a crowd of teenagers may not be where you envision yourself as a professional vocalist ten years down the road, but these are the sorts of activities you'll encounter when working with a jobbing orchestra. The more time and money spent on marketing, the more jobs will come your way. I'm always prepared for rejection—there's plenty of competition out there, no matter what kind of music you play—but the only way to succeed is to ignore it and move on to the next opportunity.

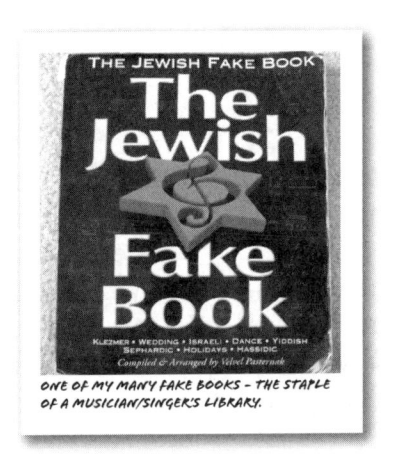

ONE OF MY MANY FAKE BOOKS - THE STAPLE OF A MUSICIAN/SINGER'S LIBRARY.

Day 3 JANUARY 18

PREDICTIONS
- E-mail tonight's set list to the piano player
- Scan Craig's List for job opportunities

DIARY
Even though I could bring tonight's set list with me, I decide to e-mail it to my piano player first thing this morning. That will give him a chance to sort out the tunes we're performing. Even so, it's likely we'll deviate from the list at some point during the evening, whether to fulfill a special request or simply because we feel like it. I always carry with me a large book with hundreds of tunes charted out in my singing keys. It contains the lyrics as well. Even though I have most of the words committed to memory,

it's comforting to know I can always look down if I'm in danger of stumbling over a phrase. But I don't use this book for my rock-and-roll gigs. Since many of those songs are loud and fast and the lyrics are often the least important thing people listen for, if I blank out on the words I'll often substitute the names of vegetables. Words like "asparagus" and "cauliflower" can be stretched out and mumbled well enough to sound like actual lyrics. It's all in the delivery. If I sing these phrases with conviction, then no one is likely to notice that what I'm singing make no sense at all. It's true.

Along with my own material, my pianist will bring what is known as a fake book. This series of books are a staple to any jobber's library, offering condensed versions of every song you can imagine, generally divided up by genre or artist. They'll include a song's chords and key changes and sometimes a lead sheet, which is where the melody line is written out. Instrumentalists rarely need a lead sheet, but for vocalists they're mandatory if you're hoping to sing a song you don't already know. So long as you can read music, or "sight sing," you're able to oblige whatever request your audience might throw your way. Learning to sight sing is a difficult skill to master, but it's one any serious singer needs in order to be successful, especially in studio situations. If you're recording a jingle, the producer and the client don't want to pay for take after take just because you can't read the written music. By demonstrating your capacity to sight sing you increase the likelihood of being rehired.

I need to bring an invoice along with me to tonight's gig.

SHEET MUSIC FROM THE "JEWISH FAKE BOOK".

This will be our first performance for this client, and they asked us to provide them with an invoice to ensure prompt payment. Any future gigs will be billed via mail prior to the gig, as the program director prefers. That's a bit unusual, but it's great when a client wants to pay us immediately. After making up the invoice on my computer, I log onto Craig's List to check for available jobs. The key words I search include "musicians," "talent," "creative," "event," and the various TV and radio categories. Ads for musicians typically involve people who are looking to join a band, and I'll occasionally run across an ad posted by someone I know. I find it fascinating to read how they describe themselves and their ability. The anonymity of boards like Craig's List does offer room for embellishment, but I've found it pays to be as honest as possible about where your capabilities lie. Also, you should exercise a degree of caution when answering these kinds of ads. With the availability of Pro Tools and other recording software, there has been an explosion of home studios and do-it-yourself recording projects. I won't visit some guy in his basement whom I met over the Internet. If the project is in an actual studio, I'm happy to check it out. I dig up a few ads that sound interesting, with people looking for a singer or for voiceover talent. I respond with an e-mail message and suggest they check out my MySpace music page, which has a number of MP3 demos linked to it.

LESSONS/PROBLEMS

Sight singing is a very valuable skill in this business. I should find time to practice it, especially since I have some study books on the subject. There are a fair number of singing jobs out there, if you know where to look. Marketing yourself through networking sites such as MySpace has its advantages, but caution is important whenever you're meeting someone for the first time. I like to bring a friend along for these initial get-togethers. If the offer is a legitimate one, the person looking to hire you shouldn't mind.

Day 4 JANUARY 19

PREDICTIONS
- *Do microphone research on the Shure Web site*
- *Check out eBay for available mics up for bid*

DIARY
After last night's gig, I decide it's time to buy a new microphone. I'm currently using an Electro-Voice from their N/Dyme series, the model EV457. I've had this one since 1989 and love how it performs. It's what commonly known as a "singer's mic" because it's hot on the high end, which means it has a bright, shiny sound. There are a lot of low-end microphones on the market that make your voice sound muddy or muffled, no matter how good the mix may be coming out of the soundboard. I bought this mic back when I was singing with my college band. We purchased an entire p.a. system from Electro-Voice. For most of the intervening years I've insisted on using it at every gig, especially in new places since you have no idea whose lips or saliva may have come in contact with the one in the bar or tavern. Many singers practically "eat" the mic, which is why I'm so concerned about that situation. My orchestra leader doesn't supply mics for the singers, so we always bring our own. As far as our rock band goes, we use the same sound company for every gig and they wipe the mics with alcohol swabs right before we use them.

Five or six years ago, my mic really began to show its age.

THE NEW SHURE BETA 87A, MY SECOND MICROPHONE IN 20 YEARS.

I shipped it back to the factory for refurbishing, and it was returned to me almost as good as new. My orchestra leader is not a fan of my mic because of its bright sound, which requires a more time-consuming sound check for a less-experienced audio engineer. Because the orchestra does not have a dedicated soundman on staff, it falls to our leader to make the adjustments. As a result, he's been after me for several years to buy a new microphone. Two summers ago my rock band was working with a different sound company than our current one, and they had a variety of mics by Shure Brothers, which is perhaps the leader in microphone technology. They stock separate mics for various kinds of instruments, and singing through one specifically made for vocals will sound different than using a mic made for a kick drum, for example. I sampled three different Shure mics—the SM87, the Beta 87A, and the wireless SLX system attached to the Beta 87A. Going wireless has its

TESTING OUT ONE OF THE SHURE MICS AT AN OUTDOOR GIG WHILE 9 MONTHS PREGNANT (AND MY ALMOST 2YR. OLD AT MY FEET!).

advantages, as your movement on stage is unrestricted. But there's a tradeoff, including increased cost and the risk of interference. One time I was performing at a downtown hotel, and suddenly the voice of a taxicab dispatcher came across our sound system. Broadcast frequencies can overlap. With so many wireless devices in use these days—especially those employing Bluetooth technology—you're constantly at risk for all sorts of interference. Finally, a wired connection will always give you the best sound, even if it's only a minor improvement over a wireless one.

Taking everything into consideration, I preferred the Beta 87A. After last night's gig, when a piece of the electronics came out when I disconnected the mic cable, I realized it was time for an upgrade. I decide to check out Shure's Web site to see if they have any newer models on hand. A detailed examination of their line convinces me that the Beta

PREGNANT AND SINGING AT AN ORCHESTRA GIG WITH MY OLD ELECTRO VOICE 457 MICROPHONE.

87A remains my best option. Then I log onto eBay to see if anyone is selling one for below the suggested retail price. I don't happen to find a private party with this model for sale, but I do locate an online audio dealer with the mic at a "best offer" price. That's where you name the price you're willing to pay, and the dealer can respond if the quote is acceptable. When dealing on this level, you have to be careful that the seller is willing to accept a re-bid if your first offer gets turned down. Otherwise you lose out altogether or are forced to select the higher "buy it now" price. I submit my offer and will wait for the seller to respond. According to eBay's rules, the seller has up to forty-eight hours to accept or decline the offer.

LESSONS/PROBLEMS
Knowing about your gear is a valuable tool in ensuring your voice gets its best possible exposure. Valuable information

can be gleaned from other singers, people who work at music stores, and from researching details on the Internet. There's an abundance of information out there, and it pays to do your homework when it comes to buying the instrument through which your voice will be heard by the world. It's tempting to cut corners, but a good microphone will pay off in the end. I'm not talking about going crazy and purchasing a microphone for a thousand dollars. But as you start testing mics in all sorts of price ranges, it soon becomes obvious that there's a great deal of difference between a $59 unit and one that costs $250.

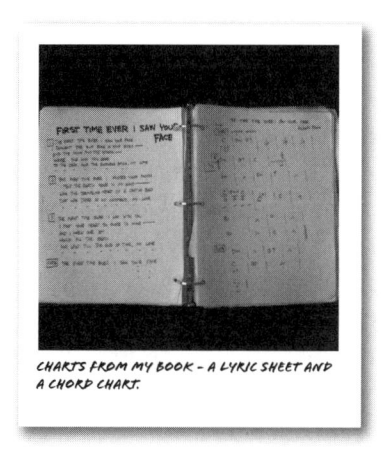

CHARTS FROM MY BOOK - A LYRIC SHEET AND A CHORD CHART.

Day 5 JANUARY 20

PREDICTIONS
- *Repair my orchestra books*
- *Perform at a bar mitzvah*

DIARY

Today I have a 12:15 hit at a synagogue in one of Chicago's North Shore suburbs, a forty-minute trip from my house. That means I'll show up no later than five past noon to get myself ready for the performance that begins at a quarter past the hour. Vocalists have it pretty easy in these circumstances. Unlike drummers or keyboard players, we don't have a ton of gear to set up, which makes arriving an hour early unnecessary. I have a good-sized book of tunes I bring to every gig. I also bring along four books that have the charts for the musicians to read. My personal book has charts for pretty much all the instruments, plus the lyrics. Charts can be expensive. A lead sheet will run $5–$10, while a fully scored piece that includes all the chord changes can cost as much as $35. Fortunately our orchestra's bass player makes charts for me for free. I always try to get him to accept payment, which he refuses, so I'll usually bring him a treat or a restaurant gift card. When I first started out in this business, the bandleader paid me in charts for my first few gigs. I've also collected charts over the years from other singers. There's nothing wrong with sharing charts, but you don't want to ask the same people over and over if you can have copies of certain songs, especially if they had to pay for them. However, most chart writers are willing to sell you a chart inexpensively if it's already on file. A chart that costs $30 to generate may only run you a few dollars. And with the development of new software, you can transpose a chart into a different key with the touch of a button. With all the use they get, my books get pretty beat up. I go through them, page by page, and make the necessary repairs. Holes are reinforced and torn pages are taped back together. I keep all my songs in alphabetical order by title, so anytime I add something new I find it's necessary to rearrange the pages. For me, it's still the best way to find a song in a hurry, though.

Most orchestras keep their tunes in some sort of numerical order, and the leader tells his players what's next by signaling the number with one or both hands. Hand signals are used because it's close to impossible to hear someone call out the number over all the instruments that are playing, not to mention fairly unprofessional. Leaders rarely program their sets ahead of time. The order in which songs are played is often changed based on the vibe in the room. Part of the leader's job is to gauge the audience's temperament. You may begin a set with some Sinatra favorites but, if no one gets up to dance halfway through the first song, it's vital to change the groove as a way of getting people on their feet. When you're dealing with players of a certain caliber, the leader can flash a hand signal and everyone will switch to the new music in a nearly seamless manner. In their haste to get to the next song, musicians often turn the pages roughly and tear them a bit. When the pages are barely hanging on, you know it's time to dig out the adhesive tape and the reinforcement grommets. After fixing up my four books, which takes me several hours, I check to see if my eBay offer has been accepted. There's no response, so I resolve to check again after I return home from my gig.

Today's performance is a pretty straightforward bar mitzvah, with no surprises. We begin with the hora, a traditional Israeli circle dance with a tune nearly everyone has heard, and then switch to background music while the guests eat their lunch. On Saturdays we're pretty limited as to what we're allowed to play in a synagogue. Secular music is usually out so I'll sing some Israeli love songs, and the orchestra loads up on folk tunes and line dances. Under these circumstances nearly everything I sing has lyrics in Hebrew, Yiddish, or Ladino, which is the language of Sephardic Jews from before the Inquisition and a mix of

A COMPUTER-GENERATED CHART.

Hebrew and Spanish. If the house of worship happens to belong to the Reform movement, which is the least restrictive when it comes to adhering to the rules of Judaism, we're free to widen our play list to Motown, rock-and-roll, and so on. This particular place isn't officially a Reform temple, but they're relatively lenient so it's possible to mix in some non-secular music. Because my orchestra leader is a member of the congregation here, we play at quite a few of their parties. Everyone always seems appreciative of our efforts, willing to participate in nearly all the folk and line dances we perform. As the party comes to a close, we play a few Sinatra tunes for the older guests who are still there, and close with a disco song for the youngsters.

LESSONS/PROBLEMS
Singers in jobbing orchestras find it absolutely vital to show up with a chart book or, at the very least, a list of all the

tunes you know and the keys in which you can sing them. Sometimes you'll come across an ensemble with a three- or four-piece horn section, and they'll have charts specifically with their parts. Whenever the leader calls out those tunes, you really can't expect them to transpose on the fly, so either you'll have to sing it in the key the charts were written in, or else ask the leader to select something else. If you're singing with a smaller group that doesn't have horn players, it's usually easier for string players to change keys on the spot. Having your own book in your keys will come in handy, especially if you have tunes other leaders want to perform that they don't have in their own books.

OUR STAND COVERED IN BLACK FABRIC TO ACCOMMODATE THE BRIDE AND GROOM.

Day 6 *JANUARY 21*

PREDICTIONS
- *Rest my voice*
- *Take care of several requests for a February wedding*

DIARY
During the winter, Sunday is generally a very slow day for performers, with relatively few gigs on the schedule. The cold, unpredictable weather may be one cause of this, but financial recovery from the holidays is probably another reason. Vendors such as hotels, florists, photographers, and musicians are willing to reduce their fees because winter is "off-season." Summer can be incredibly busy, with as many as four gigs every weekend. You need well-paying days like those to balance out the leaner months of January and

February, when you may be lucky to have any gigs at all. During this slow period I work hard on the marketing side, on behalf of our rock band as well as for my own studio and commercial projects. I try to take advantage of Sundays to rest my voice. Vocal rest applies not only to singing, but to talking as well. It means keeping as quiet as you can. The last thing a singer needs is to develop swollen nodules on their vocal cords. Left untreated, they can turn into career-ending polyps. Speech therapy can be very useful to a singer, along with keeping your throat hydrated and rested as much as possible.

I have a few tasks to look after for the wedding our band will soon play. First I need to find a couple of special-request songs, one for a father-daughter dance and another for a mother-son dance. These are two pieces I don't have on CD, so the easiest solution is to buy them online from iTunes at a buck apiece. Also, the bride and groom have asked us to alter the appearance of our music stands. Whenever we play private affairs such as weddings or fancy corporate parties, we leave our huge backdrop at home—the one with the name of our band on it—and our drummer replaces his logo-heavy bass drum head with a plain white one. Meanwhile, our black music stands have the band's name and logo printed on the front of them. Every group I know does this, since it doesn't make sense to announce your name to a private audience the same way you might when playing in a bar. It's a distinctly low-key way to have people remember the name of your group and, you hope, hire you for one of their own functions. This particular client, however, feels that the logo is too informal for their wedding. They would prefer us to use plain stands or no stands at all, or else cover up the logo so it's invisible to the audience. Playing without stands is clearly not an option. We need them to hold our music books to perform the pieces we haven't committed to memory. I need my stand to support the schedule of events for the evening, along with the names of the bridal party and the speech-givers. Substitution won't work, since we all own different kinds of stands that aren't uniform in appearance. That leaves only one option—cover up the logo. I drag one of our stands to a fabric store, figuring I can find some black material opaque enough to hide the logo when light is shining on it. It's also important to find something lightweight enough to keep the stand from tipping over. The clerk suggests a dense, black silk, and it seems to be perfect for the job. It's also an inexpensive fix, as I need only one linear yard to cover all four stands.

LESSONS/PROBLEMS

Singers should always be aware of their instrument. Unlike an athlete, who can easily tell if he or she is injured, a singer may find that more difficult to detect. Vocal fatigue occurs for any number of reasons. Does your voice sound "tired" only rarely, or is it a regular occurrence? Hearing a whoosh of air can be a sign that the vocal cords aren't sealing properly, which calls for a professional evaluation. Rest and proper hydration are the two best things you can do for your voice. When leading a band, there are always challenges from your clients. The ability to find a creative and inexpensive solution is a win-win situation. At first I was annoyed when my clients asked me to cover up our stands, but I'm glad I took the time to figure out a reasonable solution. After all, it's their big day and I wouldn't want them to feel as if we couldn't oblige their every request, no matter how odd.

ROCK-AND-ROLL CLUB DATE.

Day 7 *JANUARY 22*

PREDICTIONS
- *Watch for a reply on my eBay offer*
- *Set up a meeting with the February wedding client*

DIARY
The eBay seller has rejected my offer for the Shure microphone, but I'm able to place another bid. His asking price is already a good deal, around $50 less than retail. I make another offer, at $20 under his asking price, and we'll see what he says. As long as I can continue to make offers, it can't hurt to try. Even paying the seller his full asking price would save me money.

The wedding gig I'm planning came from one of my favorite

agents. He used to book our band in several music clubs around town and has really seen our group evolve over the years. He has his own booking agency now and manages to finds us several weddings and corporate holiday parties a year, now that we're actively soliciting that kind of business. He does my jazz quartet bookings as well. These particular clients saw us play at a bar mitzvah back in November, and they chose us over another band this agent also handles. Negotiations with the groom followed, and the first question he asked was what sort of discount they could expect since it was a February event, not a prime time for weddings. Suddenly I knew these would be difficult clients to satisfy. The price we'd quoted was already on the low end, and we weren't even charging extra for the downtown venue. Most bands charge a premium for downtown gigs to cover parking fees, which can run as high as $25.00 a vehicle. After the agent explained this to the groom, he said a friend would play the guitar during the cocktail hour and then "spin" some CDs during dinner. As a result, they only need us to play for three hours of dancing after dinner is over. There is a standard as to how things are done in this business. If you're hired for a three-hour gig that begins at nine o'clock, the job ends at midnight—otherwise overtime charges kick in. Unless you're asked to play continuously, for which there is an additional fee, the band will take two paid breaks during those three hours. The groom assumed we'd start at nine and play until 12:30 or 12:45, with no overtime charge. It's not how many minutes you play, however, but instead how long you're there once the gig begins. The meter starts the second we play our first note. Even then we're not charging for the time the musicians and the soundman are there early, several hours ahead, to perform their sound checks. It's this sort of attitude that gives jobbing musicians a bad a taste for playing weddings.

I send the groom an e-mail message to arrange a time to meet with him and his fiancée so we can discuss the particulars of their big night. I'm already aware of their two special dance requests and their concern about our logo on the music stands. I'll need to know what they want us to play for their first dance as husband and wife, whether there will be a bridal party dance, and any other requests they may have. I'd like this meeting to take place by the end of January, since the band will rehearse no later than February 2 to finalize our sets for this wedding. Most jobbing bands don't work from set lists, but my rock band is different. These guys are veterans of the bar scene, having played in various rock bands over the years. I'll make up the sets for the wedding, and the guys will organize their charts exactly that way. All their other charts will be kept in alphabetical order in case I stray from the original set, based on the reactions of the partygoers. At that point I go to each of them and call out the title of the next tune, or else point to it on their set lists. If I want to perform a song not part of the original set, I'll find the proper page in my book and hold it up for them to see. It would be great if we could all commit every song to memory, but that's an almost impossible goal.

LESSONS/PROBLEMS
Leading a band takes patience—with your players, many

kinds of clients, and yourself. Having been a sideman in an orchestra, I know how ugly "leader-itis" can be. I also realize the value in placating bridal parties and their parents. After all, it's their big day and they're nervous about all sorts of things. That hardly justifies some of the difficulties I've dealt with over the years, but those stories are for another time.

A PAST SINGER SPOTLIGHT JR. SHOW FLYER.

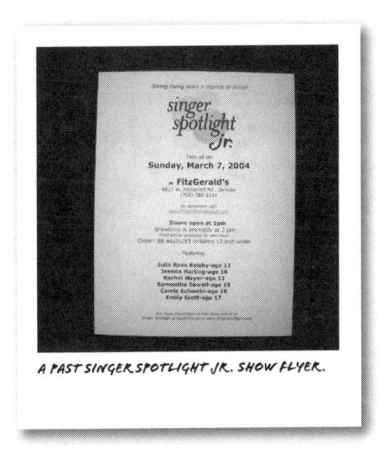

Day 8 JANUARY 23

PREDICTIONS
- *Contact singers for my February showcase*

DIARY
Four times a year I host and produce a showcase for singers, and twice a year we do a juniors' show that features performers under the age of 18. Today I'll contact the four people who've been selected to perform. We levy a cover charge at our show—the money pays the musicians and the soundman—but it's not designed to be a moneymaking enterprise. The concept allows singers to perform in front of a live audience, accompanied by professional studio musicians. Singers can choose to perform original material or else cover someone else's songs. When I first began

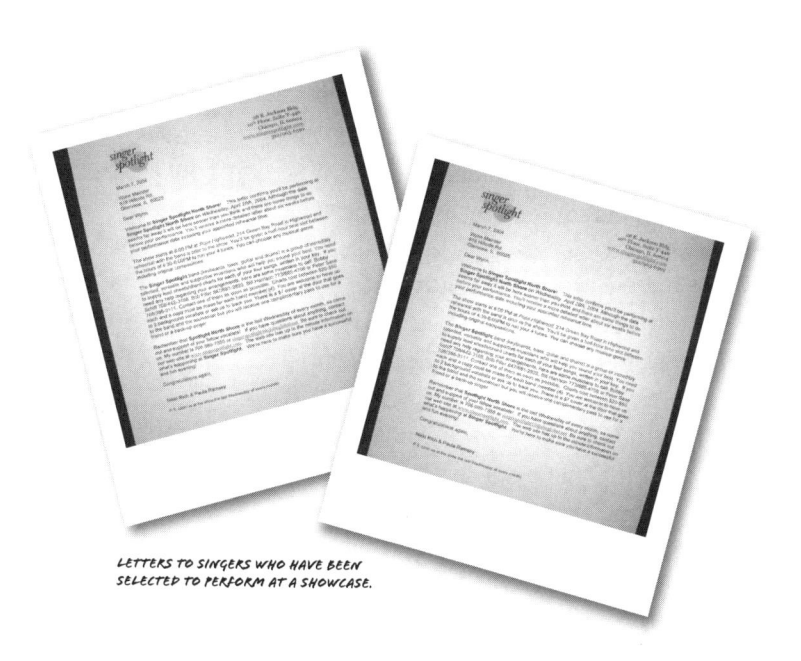

LETTERS TO SINGERS WHO HAVE BEEN SELECTED TO PERFORM AT A SHOWCASE.

performing at these showcases, more than a decade ago, I used it as an opportunity to sing four songs I didn't normally perform. These showcases are also good for networking with other singers, and they offer a chance to be heard by some of the best studio and jobbing musicians in the city. Orchestra leaders also frequent these shows to locate new talent they may not have heard before.

Four singers show up late in the afternoon for a brief rehearsal with the house band, and then it's show time. The emcee kicks things off by greeting the audience and explaining the show's format. Two singers each perform their four songs, followed by an intermission. The showcase closes with the final two singers performing their four songs. Each singer is responsible for bringing readable charts to rehearsal, and they're also strongly encouraged to pack the audience with their friends and relatives. The show's organizer selects the order in which the singers appear, oftentimes determined by listening to audition tapes. I'll generally place a "weaker" singer first, closing the first half of the show with someone stronger. But sometimes it makes sense to trot out your two best singers at the end, since it's important to keep the club filled as long as possible.

My next show is on February 28, so today I send out e-mails to each of the four singers. The message includes a reminder to send along their song lists and biographical information at least two weeks beforehand. It's important that there should be no duplicate songs on the schedule, and having this list also assists me in deciding the order of performance. I'm the host, so I get to open and close the show with a song. It's just as important that neither of my selections clash with those of the opening or closing singers. I may even pick something that complements their four-song sets, if that's possible. We maintain a Web site for the showcase, and I find it boosts attendance if we post our upcoming singers' bios early.

Because we're settling into a new venue, one of the considerations involved each singer's ability to draw an audience. The woman I've tentatively chosen to open the show is a first-timer to the showcase scene. She has a nice-sounding voice—relatively unseasoned, but that's all right. The main concept of the showcase is to give novice performers a chance to work on their stage skills and polish their public persona. We can usually rely on first-timers to bring in a large crowd of friends and family for support, which definitely helps the evening's receipts. Two of the other singers are showcase veterans. One of them is an especially capable singer who lives in the area and always draws a large crowd of admirers. The other veteran is a serious session singer whose voice has been heard in numerous national commercials. Because she lives in the neighborhood as well, I expect she'll attract quite a few people. The fourth singer performed for us once before. Her day job is nearby, and her singing is more a hobby than a vocation. Once I hear back from the singers about the programs they plan to perform, I'll finalize the singing order for the evening.

I also e-mail my band to remind them of the show we have coming up, asking them to confirm their availability. Doing this now gives me enough time to locate a substitute in the event someone can't make it.

LESSONS/PROBLEMS
As often happens with young and/or novice singers, getting the wrong idea about these showcases is harmful when they truly can be a great boost to a budding career. These shows are meant to improve your self-confidence and help you find your comfort zone on stage. It's a support system in which every singer takes part. Many of these shows act as introductions to the people with whom you'll eventually work in various jobbing and recording sessions. The singers will lend you their charts and ask you to sub for them. It's an excellent networking opportunity, and one not to be missed.

THE SPRA BOOKLET FROM THE TRADE SHOW.

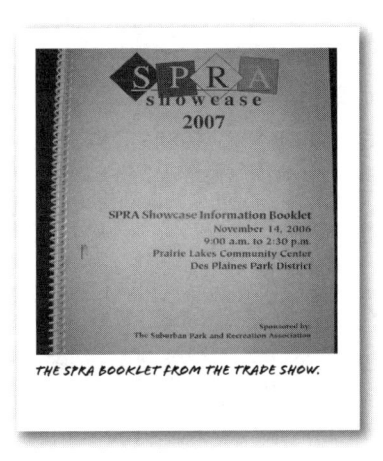

Day 9 JANUARY 24

PREDICTIONS
- Check with park district for summer shows
- Contact new agencies

DIARY
Several months ago I attended a trade show sponsored by Illinois park districts and recreation centers. These folks gather every November to collect ideas for their upcoming summer's entertainment. In past years our band participated through an independent agent, but I finally decided it was worth the $45 table fee for us to be there in person—greeting the attendees and blowing our own horn, you might say. We brought along demo CDs, promotional kits, and other giveaways, and behind the table we posted a

photomontage of the various performances we'd done over the past few years. I made sure that everyone who picked up our material dropped off a business card. Even though these are not high-paying gigs, it's a great way to get people to notice us in various communities around town, and it's really fun to perform outdoors in the summer. Today I spend close to an hour making follow-up calls to the people whose business cards I'd collected, but I only manage to reach one live person—all my other efforts end up in voice-mail. I send out e-mail as a backup, reminding each of them of our interest in performing for their district. Past experience tells me I'll receive very few responses, since most people aren't comfortable acknowledging that they've booked another band in your place. It can be disheartening to receive such minimal return for all the time and money that's put into promoting the band, but I try not to take it personally. While it's always possible that someone may simply not like the type of music you play, there are plenty of other reasons why you don't get hired. As far as these summer concerts are concerned, they may already have another band in the series that covers similar material as yours, or perhaps you played for them last summer and they have a policy of not booking the same group two years in a row.

The trade show's program lists all the exhibiting entertainers and their representative agencies. Half a dozen agents paid for display ads, and I see we're only listed with one of them. But before I contact them, I visit each agency's Web site to see what sort of bands they're already representing, and which venues they book. By doing my homework, I'm able

KEN, JOHN GRIFFIN (OUR LEAD GUITAR PLAYER) AND ME AT A SUMMER CONCERT.

to weed out several agencies that are not a good fit for us. The remaining agents I either call or e-mail to ask if they're accepting submissions from new bands. One of the agencies reports that they focus only on the list of artists already posted on their site. This agent is a musician who plays in several bands, and it's his intention to keep his agency business "in house."

After my calls I check out the eBay auction and discover that my price for the microphone has been accepted. I arrange for payment, knowing that the microphone will arrive in about a week. Then I repost my Craig's List ad as a session singer. There are several categories that can accommodate my listing. Those are titled "musicians" and "talent gigs," although there may be other groupings in other cities. While visiting that site I scan the ads for anything new, and I spot a notice about a company that's looking for bands to play

A SUMMER GIG.

corporate and private parties. I send them an e-mail inquiry to find out more.

LESSONS/PROBLEMS

My favorite mantra when being turned away for a gig is, "Don't take it personally." There are many reasons why someone is not selected, most of them beyond a singer's control. Sometimes the cause involves good old office politics, and you can't change that. The goal should be to stay focused on what you're trying to accomplish. Getting your name out there, or that of your band, takes determination. Persistence—tempered with restraint—is a mandatory trait in this industry. There's a fine balance between "brand awareness" and having people roll their eyes at the sound of your name. Competition is fierce; don't let a few rejections get you down.

Day 10 *JANUARY 25*

PREDICTIONS
- *Create a performance set list*
- *Rehearse tonight for Saturday's gig*

DIARY
Several e-mails I receive are cause for some quick action. One company regularly sends me instrumental song tracks, and I record the vocal lines over them. Today this client has asked me to sing two songs. Because the sound files are too large to transmit as an e-mail attachment, I visit an Internet FTP site to download them directly. Once I've completed my share of the work, I'll send them back the same way. There are four files in all awaiting me—two for each song—where one includes the vocal melody and the other does not. There is also a file with the lyrics, which I print out for later use. Next, I call my friend and band mate who has a recording studio located less than ten minutes from my house. I send him the FTP link and we agree to turn this project around in two or three days. I've received a second e-mail message, this one regarding voiceover work. This is a specialized field where you often see crossover between singers and voiceover artists. Many of the best voiceover people are trained actors who can do a variety of believable voices. This particular company has sent me a sample script to record, which I'll return as an MP3 file along with the rate I plan to charge per spot.

Our band is rehearsing tonight for a party at a country club, where the ages of the guests will range from early thirties through early sixties. It's important to know how old your audience will be in order to select the appropriate songs from your repertoire. Since our band got its start in the bars, the hard-driving rock-and-roll songs we know from those days are more appropriate to a private affair with guests in their twenties and thirties. Our standard repertoire includes lots of classic Motown and disco tunes, plus songs from the 1980s that inspire people to dance. Many people claim they don't want to hear what every other band plays. We've performed at parties where we've been warned away from such overplayed tunes as "I Will Survive" or "We Are Family," only to find people coming up to the bandstand and requesting them.

Most jobbing bands rarely rehearse, since all their players are accomplished sight-readers. Not all players have these skills, however. My rock band is not composed of jobbers, which is why we need to rehearse. That's also the reason I create a set list for each show. With hardcore pros I can use hand signals to indicate the key of the next song. Once they hear me sing the first few words, they'll immediately know which piece it is and jump right in. Playing in a bar or garage band is a completely different animal. In that situation, people listen to recordings and then play from memory. Ever since our bar band crossed over into the jobbing world, our sets have evolved into a hybrid of both styles. We play memorized songs from the club repertoire plus typical jobbing tunes for which we've built or borrowed music charts. These charts exist in the event someone happens to forget their part from one performance to another, although everyone who plays some music by heart has a tendency to play every song that way. The challenge involves the sheer quantity of songs this band is forced to memorize, including standards, oldies, and brand-new tunes currently on the radio.

Our keyboard player is running late again, as usual, so our rehearsal's starting time is delayed. It makes little sense to start without him, since he's also one of our vocalists. After he arrives we review the set lists and decide which songs need rehearsing. We tend to think we know material better than we actually do. We seem to flub something at least once whenever we perform in front of an audience, and I'll usually make a mental note of it for our next rehearsal. That way, as we're going down the set lists, I can point out why we need to go over a song when the rest of the band doesn't think we need the practice. After our session I bring up the topic of adding a second keyboard player to the group. I believe this would allow us to cover more instrumentation, such as a four-piece horn section, with a single player. Also, our regular keyboardist likes to play rhythm guitar on some songs, so we wouldn't be without that instrument whenever he picks up the guitar.

LESSONS/PROBLEMS
As with many aspects of life, lack of time is a huge problem. I'd like to record a worthwhile voiceover demo tape, but I never seem to get to it. What I should do is create several fake ads, or else transcribe the ones I hear on the radio

and use them as my material. Voiceover work is amazingly competitive, but it can be quite lucrative. I could also stand to learn some new songs, since every week there's another hot new tune on the radio—if only there was more time.

A NEW WEB SITE HOME PAGE UNDER CONSTRUCTION.

Day 11 JANUARY 26

PREDICTIONS
- Advance our discussion for a new band member
- Check on the progress of our Web site
- Order more band stationery

DIARY
One of our showcase singers is dropping out of our February production, so I need to find a replacement. The challenge here is to sign up a singer who performs similar music as well as one who can pull in a crowd. The woman who needs replacing performs "pop" and Broadway show tunes, and she's always been a big draw for us. I'll call my co-producer to see if she knows of a likely candidate. Time is short, and we need to move fast to line up a new singer and give that

person both a chance to prepare and also to put out the word to their fan base.

During last evening's rehearsal, I brought up the subject of finding a second keyboard player for the band. A skilled keyboardist can produce a large number of sounds—not just piano and organ, but also horn and string parts, synthesizer sounds, and nearly endless samples of just about any instrument on the planet. The first time I suggested it our regular keyboard guy got very defensive, insisting all we needed was some new equipment to help him cover the sounds we needed for various songs. That discussion took place quite a few months ago, and nothing's changed. Now we're serious about adding songs to our repertoire that will require greater sound variety, plus I know he still wants to do backup vocals and play rhythm guitar every so often. After a night of sleeping on it, I'm pleased to see a number of positive e-mail responses from my band mates. Everyone agrees that it makes sense to add another player—even thought that would cut into the share each of us makes—in order to improve the overall sound of the band. Even our current keyboard player understands that we're hiring someone to help him out rather than replace him. Our next step involves posting an ad on Craig's List and several other musicians-wanted bulletin boards.

I send a follow-up e-mail to our designer, checking on the progress of our new Web site. He's promised to have some pages ready for my review by the end of the week. I also send an e-mail message to our printer. I'm looking for an

PROMO MATERIAL OF THE BAND THAT INCLUDES OUR DEMO CD.

updated listing of the artists whose songs we cover, and also some blank pages I use for letter writing. Our stationery uses a large ship's wheel as a background image—sort of like a watermark—as well as pictures along the bottom of the sheet with shots from the "Gilligan's Island" television show. With more than three hundred marketing kits to send out to various agencies and potential clients, I'll need a lot of letterhead on hand.

I see Craig's List shows that yet another agency is looking to add new voiceover talent to their stable, so I bookmark the page for future reference. I'm taping a demo disk next Monday, so I'll send one to them as soon as it's finished.

LESSONS/PROBLEMS
I've learned that it's not the end of the world whenever a musician cancels. Everyone can be replaced—even me—and

THE DESK IN MY HOME OFFICE.

it's important to keep one's head in those situations. Also, egos are a very delicate thing. This whole situation about adding a second keyboard player was initially threatening to our band's existing one. A good bandleader makes sure that musicians always feel valued and appreciated. I explained privately that we were concerned about his excessive workload, not his skill level or ability to perform. When he's always worried about putting the next set of sounds together in time for the next song on the list, he can't possibly enjoy making music.

PERFORMING AT A FUNDRAISER IN OUR "DRESS BLACKS."

Day 12 *JANUARY 27*

PREDICTIONS
- *Perform at a fundraising event*

DIARY
Tonight's fundraising gig was exhausting. We played an hour longer than scheduled while working the crowd and packing everything up, which seemed to take forever. This venue is a terrific one for us, and I'm hoping tonight's performance will convince the club owner to book us for a regular weekend gig soon. Part of the schmoozing I did included extended conversations with the club's employees and assistant manager. The only drawback involves the distance I have to drive, as this place is more than an hour from home. If we play a weekend night until 1:00 A.M., I won't be home until

two-thirty at the earliest. That's rough when you have two little ones who insist on rising at dawn every day. I'd still love to play this club because it has such a high profile as a live music venue. It also draws its own crowd, which means that people visit the place without regard to the group that's booked to perform that night. For our band, which has been away from the club scene for many years, this would be a great chance to get our name out there and rebuild our following.

We arrived at the place by six o'clock. By the time we did our sound check—where all the instruments and the microphones have their sound levels tested and mixed—it was 7:30 P.M., about half an hour later than expected. These people had quite a few events planned for the evening, including a silent auction, a raffle, and a video presentation on the target of their fundraising efforts—the Ronald McDonald House—followed by a buffet-style dinner and us, their live entertainment.

With everything they had on the agenda, I knew there was no way we'd stay on schedule. Experience tells me this is often the case, where things get pushed back and delayed. As the guests began to arrive, we played some easy-listening music on CD since the event's organizers wanted to keep us from distracting attendees as they walked around and placed bids on the items up for auction. The food stations were ready to go no earlier than eight o'clock, which meant we couldn't start playing dance music until close to nine. I made the decision to begin at 8:15 with some live background music, just to give us something to do. We played in this "low and slow" style for around forty minutes and then took a break while the people running the event made some introductions and showed their video. The band had something to eat, after which we returned to the stage with an increased energy level that brought people to the dance floor in droves. The raffle took place during our next break, and our third set kicked off at half past ten with lots of dance tunes and Top Forty favorites. We finished our final set at about ten past eleven, playing two extra songs since the dance floor remained packed to capacity. We left everyone wanting more, and that's what you want to do so the crowd's last thoughts about you and your band are positive.

As we tore down and packed up I handed out business cards to everyone who asked, knowing we'd never hear from more than a tiny fraction of these people. More importantly, the assistant manager thought we did a great job. He encouraged me to call their talent booker later in the week to see about scheduling us for some future weekend evening. Other than the altruistic intention of helping out at a fundraiser, this was one of my main goals in playing tonight. For the benefit of our band's future I wanted to impress the management at this club, and it appears that worked to perfection.

LESSONS/PROBLEMS
Flexibility is vital, especially for a bandleader. Party planners and event hosts have a million things on their minds, and it's important that the band doesn't leave a lasting impression of

being difficult by not accommodating last-minute requests. It's our job to make everyone as happy as possible and ensure that they're having a great time. Doing so will lead to a successful event and a positive connection with your name, which you hope will translate into more work in the future.

MARYANN GIG CHECKLIST.

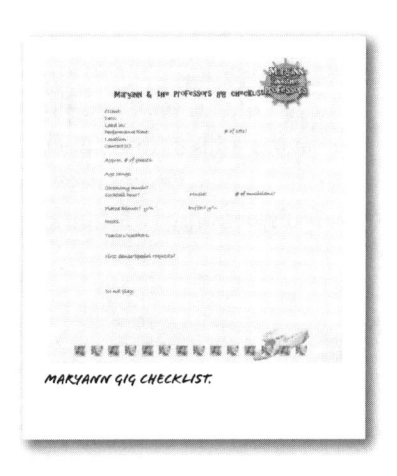

Day 13 *JANUARY 30*

PREDICTIONS
- *Meet with clients for Saturday's wedding*
- *Prepare for the rehearsal with the band*

DIARY
Today I'm meeting with the bride and groom to discuss their Saturday night wedding reception. It's disappointing that the first chance we have to discuss this event face-to-face is a mere five days before the wedding. I'll usually meet with clients at least six to eight weeks prior to the big day and then again ten days out, if necessary, to finalize the details. In this situation, part of the short notice was due to the bride and groom's delay in confirming their booking with us. I'm apprehensive about this meeting—a first in all the years I've

done this—because of all the haggling the groom did with our agent and me prior to having booked us. I drive into the city to our scheduled meeting spot, a popular coffee shop. The bride is a sweet and soft-spoken person who apparently fell in love with our band as soon as she heard our demo CD. She and I hit it off immediately as we wait for the groom to arrive.

I have a standard series of questions for clients that helps me determine which songs from our repertoire will work best for the guests expected to attend the event. It's important for a band to know its audience so it can make informed choices about what material to play. For example, if you discover that a large number of the partygoers love jam band music, it's a pretty good plan to play a lot of music by The Grateful Dead and Phish. If the bulk of the crowd will be made up of Baby Boomers, plan on plenty of classic rock by the Rolling Stones, the Beatles, Van Morrison, and so on. Obviously, you want to find out as much as you can about the couple's musical preferences—and those of the parents, especially if they're footing the bill—but it's just as important to ask about the guests. How many people are expected? What's the average age of most of the partygoers? Will there be a lot of folks over 60? The three of us chat for close to an hour about what kind of music they like, which songs they definitely don't want us to play, and how they expect the evening to run. I make a list of the people who will give toasts or speeches, their order of introduction, and the pronunciation of all their names.

A BULLS ANTHEM AT THE UNITED CENTER IN CHICAGO.

In preparation for this meeting, the couple has jotted down a list of songs they definitely want to have played at some point during the evening, circling tunes on the song list that came in our promo kit as well as adding a few pieces that weren't there. The sheer number of songs they've requested will never fit in the three sets we've agreed to play, so we do some judicious whittling down. By suggesting several titles they hadn't included, I make sure we play a little something for everyone. It's also important that we temper all the fast-paced music with a few medium tempo and slower songs. Finally, they're delighted to hear we solved the stand "problem" by draping them with black material. All in all it's a good meeting, and the groom turns out to be much more likeable in person.

LESSONS/PROBLEMS
Playing for private affairs means you must deal with all kinds

of people. In this particular instance, the bride and groom were much more pleasant than I expected. A lot of asocial behavior on the part of bridal parties can be attributed to the nervousness that goes along with planning the big day. The bandleader's job is to eliminate complications and help create a memorable event. Comply with every possible request, reassure them at every turn that they'll be throwing a great party, and smile a lot. Knowing your audience is a key element to playing a successful event. If you don't know anything about the crowd—the names of their favorite bands, which radio stations they prefer, and the type of dancing they enjoy—you'll risk ending up with inappropriate song selections. Many people place the success of an event on the band's shoulders, by having the dance floor filled all evening long and how well the musicians re-create the songs. We always give ourselves the best chance to succeed by asking as many questions as possible.

Day 14 *FEBRUARY 1*

PREDICTIONS
- *Rehearsal for Saturday's wedding*
- *Make CDs and charts for new songs to distribute at rehearsal*

DIARY

Tonight is our "tightening up" rehearsal, the one that makes sure we have all the special requests down cold for the wedding this Saturday. Earlier I'd sent the set lists out via e-mail so everyone would be prepared. In addition to the songs we made a point of learning for the bride and groom, there are several others in our repertoire that feel a bit rusty because we only perform them at weddings. We'll also work on smoothly transitioning between songs to keep the dance floor filled. We always try to segue directly from one piece to the next, since even the smallest span of silence could cause people to head back to their seats.

As soon as rehearsal is over, our bass player pulls me aside and tells me he's decided to step down from the band. He chooses not to say much beyond that, other than to add he's less happy about playing live sets and would prefer to spend more time in his home studio, where he produces demos for younger singers. He mentions he's quit his part-time gig with another band as well, although he's quick to promise that we can count on him to finish out all the jobs we've booked so far, at least until a replacement player is found. He isn't interested in learning any new material, which puts a dent in my plans to have us start playing clubs again. He's also our lead male singer and an integral element of our three-part harmony. For a long time, we were only known for having good female vocals, and some agents felt that was a drawback. When we added our bass player six years ago and our keyboard player three years later, the band's vocals became outstanding. Both guys are great singers, and we were especially lucky that our three voices blended together so well. Sometimes you have a couple of terrific singers, but their voices just don't mesh. It may be because their vibratos are at different speeds, or perhaps the vocal colors aren't all that complementary. When voices blend together well, you end up with a sweet tone and a very pleasant sound.

I can see from his face that his mind is made up, and I appreciate his willingness to stay on until we find a new player, but I'm really upset about this turn of events. Less than a month ago I spoke with each band member individually about rededicating themselves to the group, asking them if playing clubs for minimal pay was all right if it also boosted our recognition, as well as a commitment to more rehearsals. At the time he was in full agreement, so this abrupt shift in his attitude makes me think there's more he isn't sharing. After six years of playing together, he's also my friend and I care about him. He insists he'll be there to play while we're auditioning a second keyboard player, but that causes another problem. Any good keyboardist who's looking to join an established band may wish to avoid ongoing reconstruction.

LESSONS/PROBLEMS

Anyone can be replaced, but that doesn't mean it's an easy process. It will be a challenge to find a new band member who is an exceptional bass player and can also shoulder most of the male lead vocals. Our keyboard player will not be able to take over all his singing, and we still have to fill in that third part of harmony. I'm also faced with the task of updating our promo kit and changing biographical material on the band's Web site, neither of which is a cheap fix. However I choose to look at it, these are expenses I wish I didn't have to make at this time.

WORKING AT THE WEDDING WITH OUR STANDS COVERED UP.

Day 15 *FEBRUARY 3*

PREDICTIONS
- *Perform downtown at a wedding reception*

DIARY
This evening we're playing at the wedding for the couple I met with earlier in the week. The day starts with an e-mail message from our keyboard player. He's having trouble finding someone to cover his last few music students of the day—he teaches piano and guitar from home—and may therefore show up late for the gig. I can't simply call someone to replace him, although I wish I could. Since we're not a typical jobbing band that uses fake books or music charts, it would be almost impossible to slip in a jobber. He promises to show up by the time we're ready to play, but

I'll need to haul all his gear to the restaurant site. After that, the setup and sound checks must be done as well. Since no one lives all that close to him, someone will have to sacrifice a couple of hours of travel time to pick up his keyboards, guitar, and amp. We have a responsibility to the bride and groom to make sure the music portion of their evening goes smoothly. They don't need to know my keyboard player's issues, only that the band is ready to play at our agreed-upon time. Thankfully, our lead guitar player is able to pick up the stuff. With the rear seats in his vehicle folded down, everything should fit. At this moment I make an executive decision that the keyboard player's check will be slightly smaller than everyone else's. It's really not fair to the rest of the band, especially when they've managed to clear their schedules and arranged to set up on time.

I arrive at the restaurant to see that everything is progressing smoothly. Then I check on the bride and groom, who are enjoying appetizers and cocktails in a separate portion of the restaurant. They're both very happy to see me. We review a few details as to which order the toasts will take place, and then the matron of honor introduces me to the rest of the wedding party. Even though we're only providing the entertainment, I usually end up organizing everything that takes place during the reception, even down to the cutting of the wedding cake. After helping everyone to understand their respective duties, I head back to the other side of the restaurant. Alongside the dance floor, all our gear is ready to go except for the keyboardist's stool. No one can seem to figure out how to assemble it, so I grab a chair from the bar instead. Then we perform a quiet sound check, making sure all the microphones and instruments are hot. As the cocktail hour is winding down, I'm growing more and more nervous because our keyboard player has not yet arrived. We've been hired to start playing at eight o'clock, and by 7:30 he still isn't here. I call his cell phone but the call goes immediately to voice mail, and same thing happens when I ring his home number. For anyone who ends up working as a sideman, this is one of the worst things you can do to a bandleader. Being late and not calling will make any bandleader crazy. He shows up at ten to eight, explaining that all his lessons ran late. Luckily the reception is behind schedule, so there's no damage done. The bride and groom make a big entrance into the room after I introduce the other members of the bridal party to the attendees. Our band plays "Turn Me Loose" during the intro, the song from "The Blues Brothers" movie that elicits a great feel of mounting excitement. As I ask everyone to welcome them into the room as husband and wife, the couple heads to the dance floor for their first dance, which we keep short. Then each set of parents offers welcome toasts, followed by the blessing of the meal by the attending minister.Their original idea of having a friend spin CDs during dinner was shot down by the bride's parents, who felt that live music would be more appropriate. We play some low-and-slow background music during the salad course, stopping briefly as various individuals rise to offer words of praise. After the dinner plates are cleared, the bride and groom address their guests, cut the wedding cake, and then the dancing begins. We run straight down our list, starting with swingers for the older guests and then Motown tunes, followed by disco and pop selections. Before we know it, break time arrives and it's a chance for the band to grab a meal. This is one contract element I always include when we're playing a wedding—dinner for the entertainers.

We begin our next set with a variety of special requests, including the father-daughter dance and the mother-son dance. Then it's back to some high-energy party tunes, followed by our last break of the evening. The final set includes requests for some hard-rock cover pieces by AC/DC, Kiss and others, and then its eleven o'clock—the end of our contracted three hours. The groom asks if we're willing to play a bit longer, so overtime kicks in and we keep going straight through until midnight. As we're packing up our equipment, the best man hands me a check for the original total while the bride's father writes a check for the hour of overtime, plus a generous tip.

LESSONS/PROBLEMS
It's difficult for a bandleader to remain calm at live gigs—especially weddings—what with the constant pressure to perform well. Your face and voice will be forever captured on the wedding video, and you certainly don't want it to evoke a negative response. Dealing with scatterbrained musicians simply comes with the territory. It's important to remember to keep your cool, saving any criticism for after the performance is over and when you're out of the public's eye. You never want to have the bridal party or their guests see that there's a problem on stage, whether technically or emotionally.

A CLUB DATE WITH AN OLD MEMBER OF THE BAND.

Day 16 *FEBRUARY 5*

PREDICTIONS
- *Place ads for a keyboard and a bass player*
- *Talk to our bass player about his decision to leave*

DIARY
I'm anxious to chat with our bass player one last time before I place an ad to find his replacement. Part of that effort is selfishness, knowing how much work we'll have to do to bring a new band member up to speed on the depth and breadth of our repertoire. I also want to know that his decision doesn't involve something I've said or done. I'm pretty much the boss of this band, since I have the greatest amount of control over what we play. I also deal directly with agents and clients, and I look after covering all our

expenses. If his decision to leave is because of how he feels as an employee, that's something I'll need to change in my own behavior. Working as part of a small group of people requires that we all get along. With as much time as we spend in rehearsals and performances, we should enjoy making music together. If anyone chooses to leave because of the way I run the band's business, that's something I need to know.

After a forty-five minute telephone call, I'm relieved to know that our bass player's departure has nothing to do with anyone in the band on a personal or musical level. I believe him when he says it was a difficult choice to make, and I also feel he's being honest when he says it has nothing to do with anyone other than himself. He furthermore reassures me that he has no problem with the way I run the band, stating that he'd definitely tell me if that were the case. After all, we've played together for more than six years, and he would have never remained silent all this time if he was unhappy. He also vows to play gigs if we need him, insisting that I should continue to book our band as usual. He clearly understands the time and investment we've all made, and he doesn't want to see that go for nothing.

As a result of this conversation, I decide to put off advertising for his replacement. If we're running ads for both a keyboardist and a bass player, it may appear that the band is not stable. That's a sure way to dissuade a veteran player from responding. Someone who's well established in this market, the sort of person we hope to attract, is far less likely to join what may look like a start-up band. Since our bass player has agreed to play with us whenever we're auditioning a second keyboard player, it's far better to show ourselves as an intact band that's simply seeking to fill out our lineup.

I'll begin by posting online ads to two popular bulletin board sites— Nextcat and Craig's List. Nextcat is one of those online music communities, somewhat similar to MySpace, where you compose a profile, add friends, post comments, advertise shows, and download music samples. They also have pages where you can search for jobs or find a musician. Best of all, posting an ad is free, unlike advertising in the *Tribune* or various other publications around Chicago like the *Reader*.

Here's what my ad looks like:
"Established Chicago cover band looking to add second keyboard player, needed for when our keyboardist plays guitar, and also to cover parts and sounds such as horns, strings, and synthesizer. We play clubs, festivals, and parties, both private and corporate, and we have agent representation."

LESSONS/PROBLEMS

If our bass player wants to stop playing with us, I can't make him feel differently about it. At that point, it's my job to make his departure as smooth as possible. Just the thought that his leaving had something to do with our internal workings caused me to step back and examine how I treat my band mates. Do I make them feel unimportant? Do I treat their suggestions with respect? What can I do to ensure they'll want to continue making music with me as part of this group? These thoughts are rarely at the forefront of my mind, but this situation has been effectively a wake-up call for me to be more mindful of those around me.

WHAT RECORDING TRACKS LOOK LIKE ON A COMPUTER.

Day 17 *FEBRUARY 8*

PREDICTIONS
- *Review responses to my online ads for a keyboard player*
- *Record part of a song for a Web site vendor*

DIARY
Three days ago I posted several online ads for a second keyboard player, and so far I've received a dozen responses. Several can be tossed out immediately, although I'll be sure to respond to every inquiry since that's the right thing to do. I did not disclose our band's identity in the ad, but I'll direct the finalists to our Web site so they can hear our MP3 demos, see a list of the artists we cover, and read testimonials from former clients. I find it interesting that some of the respondents didn't seem to understand

STUDIO SHOT OF THE MIXING BOARD AND COMPUTERS

the text of the ad. Several people ask if we sing our own compositions, since they're interested in songwriting. There's nothing wrong with that, but I was careful to explain we're a "cover" band, which means we perform material composed by others. Did they not pay attention to what I posted, or were they so inexperienced that they didn't understand one of the most common terms in the industry? Whatever the reason, I plan to explain we're probably not the best fit for them.

Several responses include links to Web sites where these musicians have posted samples of their playing. This makes things easy for me, since I can immediately weed out the lesser players before wasting their time and ours with a live audition. I forward these links to everyone else in the band, asking them for their evaluation as well. Two other people can be turned down right away since they're looking for a band that works full time, performing at least twice a week.

We don't care to be quite that busy, since each of us is involved in outside projects. Four times a month is plenty for us, although perhaps a bit more often during the summer. At this point I've whittled the list down to three potential interviewees, based upon their stated experience as to the places they've played, the bands they've been in, and the songs they've covered. In addition to providing them with our URL, I outline our band's history and explain our short- and long-term goals. I also let them know we'll schedule a live audition if we decide to move forward. I make certain to ask each of them if they sing, since it's always good to have an extra vocalist in the band. I e-mail my findings to the rest of the band and then run through the Craig's List ads to see if there are any recording opportunities for me. I'm amazed by how many people use this free service. The ad I ran three days ago is already more than four hundred places back from the most current listings. If this first batch of applicants falls flat, I'll re-post the ad to gain a more current placement.

I start up the built-in music player on my PC and open the file that contains the new song I've been asked to record. Then I print out the lyrics so I can bring them along to the recording studio. I prefer to listen while I'm doing other work so I can familiarize myself with the music. As I turn back to Craig's List to review the ads, I listen to the song over and over to help ingrain it into my temporary memory. I respond to a couple that is looking for a band to play at their wedding next fall. This is the first time I've used this site in this way, assuming people's budgets are limited if they choose this method to select a band. The place where they're holding their reception—Navy Pier—is an expensive place to book for private events, so I may have to revise my thinking on this one. I respond with an invitation to visit our band's Web site, listen to music samples, and view the list of artists we cover. It should be interesting to see if anything comes of this. If we get a gig out of it, that's great. If not, I only wasted thirty seconds of my day in answering the ad.

I grab my lyrics sheet and the CD with the song I'm about to record and head for the studio. Once that's done and I'm back home, I'll post it on the FTP site and let the vendor know the file is ready to be downloaded.

LESSONS/PROBLEMS
Finding a new player for the band is not much different than dating. There are first impressions and reactions to physical appearance, even though looks shouldn't matter. Not long ago I had an agent hold up our promo photo and point to a grey-haired, bespectacled member of our band, declaring that his college-age audiences didn't want to see that at clubs. I was shocked to discover that the quality of one's playing would be secondary to one's appearance, but that's really no different than any other aspect of the entertainment industry. At any rate, searching for that perfect musical match is nearly as challenging as finding that "special someone" with whom to share your life. Compatibility issues abound, including the ability to get along as individuals and work well together as band mates.

Day 18 *FEBRUARY 9*

PREDICTIONS
- *Prepare I.R.S. paperwork to send to band members*
- *Put together figures for a meeting with our accountant*

DIARY

As an employer who pays my musicians for each gig we play, I'm required to issue Form 1099s that report the amount of money they receive throughout the year. Whenever we work for a park district or through an independent agent, checks are made out to me rather than in the name of the band. I deposit these payments into my own account and then write checks against them to everyone who contributed to the performance. By filing copies of these 1099s with the federal government, I'm declaring that I didn't keep the entire payment. These forms are supposed to be postmarked no later than the end of January, but I'm hopeful this slight delay in sending them out won't cause any problems. The easiest way I've found to arrive at everyone's totals is to flip through my checkbook register and add up all the numbers for each payee. Anyone who earns more than $600.00 in a calendar year is required to receive a 1099.

After returning from the post office where I mailed the forms, I begin the task of putting together all my material for our accountant. I received a W2 from a part-time job I worked earlier in the year, plus a pile of 1099s from various park districts, bandleaders, and agents. Then there is a

SOME OF MY TAX WRITE-OFFS — THE DEMO CD AND INSIDE COVER.

long list of other paid gigs—almost always from private parties—for which we received payment by cash or personal check. To prepare for my meeting in a few days I collect copies of last year's return, all of this year's forms, and my list of expenses and additional deductions. Self-employed contractors can write off a whole slew of things that help reduce the amount of taxes to be paid, including anything related to my business as a singer. I save the receipts from parking garages and from clothing I've purchased specifically for performances, plus related dry cleaning costs. Any money I spend on CDs or songs I download from iTunes that I need to learn for a gig can be deducted. Every cost associated with the creation of our promo kits—duplicating expenses, CD copying, photograph printing, and the postage to mail them—needs to be tallied as well. Since my cell phone serves as my primary business contact, part of my monthly bill can be written off, too. My list of deductions is fairly long, including the cost of office supplies, a portion of our Internet access fee, meals related to band gigs, and a cost per mile for traveling to and from performances. Any purchase of equipment, such as my new microphone, also qualifies. Last year's major cost involved the initial production of our promotional kits, so related expenses for last year encompassed only a few necessary updates. We've retained a new accountant, so it will take some time to talk her through all this paperwork. I'll be sure to bring along last year's tax return for use as a template.

LESSONS/PROBLEMS

In preparation for filing the year's tax forms, it's important to save all business-related receipts plus anything else associated with one's music business. Everything purchased for self-promotion or the improvement of skills can be written off against the income you make. Self-employed individuals need to do an extra-good job of money management, since checks received as payment for gigs don't have anything deducted from them. If you spend every dime you make, you won't have anything set aside to pay the government when tax time rolls around. Keeping all your receipts handy to document your expenses is particularly helpful, especially if you get audited. While you're allowed to balance expenses against earnings, showing a loss year after year as a vocalist will serve as a red flag to the I.R.S., and that's a situation to avoid at all cost.

RICHARD DIRKES-JACKS, OUR NEW KEYBOARD PLAYER.

Day 19 *FEBRUARY 11*

PREDICTIONS
- *Set up auditions for a keyboard player*
- *Start search for a bass player*

DIARY
Two of the three keyboard players selected from those who responded to my ad have agreed to the next step in the hiring process. One appears especially suited to our situation based upon his playing experience, plus he sent along photographs of himself up on stage. These are not your typical "rock-star-poser" shots but instead straightforward pictures where he's playing a club date. The pictures show off his gear as well as the fact he can sing. Experience has taught me that a great player who employs antiquated

equipment will not sound all that good. Conversely, with all the sounds and instrument parts a keyboard can mimic, upgraded gear can make a significant difference when it comes to how well the whole group performs. He mentions he's heard of our band and also likes what he heard on our Web site. He would prefer to play no more than six times a month, which would be an improvement over his current cover band that seems to spend all its time in rehearsal. I'm delighted to learn that, like our current keyboardist, he also plays the guitar.

The second respondent also has a lot of experience, and he asserts his desire to play every gig we book rather than simply serve as a stand-in for the times our primary keyboardist is absent. His comments seem a bit presumptuous at this stage, but that's one of the risks of e-mail—the inability to discern someone's tone or intent. He's also a singer and wishes to obtain a list of our songs so he can let us know which material he already knows. I reply to both prospects with an attachment of our song list, explaining which pieces we'd like them to prepare for the audition. I copy my band mates on my e-mails, asking them to let me know which nights are good for them to help with the process. It would be best if we could audition both players on the same night.

I've decided to accept the reality of our bass player's resignation, so I'll keep my promise by beginning a search for an immediate replacement. First I decide to check out the ads that have already been posted, and it's amazing to

ANOTHER PHOTO OF RICHARD HE SUBMITTED TO US PRIOR TO HIS AUDITION.

see how many bands are seeking bass players. It's been that way for as long as I can remember, with bass players far less prevalent than lead guitar players. In the section where players are looking for bands, I find three or four players with potential. I contact them via e-mail to see if they're still on the market, and I provide a brief overview of what music we play, how often we perform, and where our pay scale lies. I also ask each of them if they can sing. Losing our bassist is a double blow because of all the singing he does, both lead and harmony.

LESSONS/PROBLEMS

Keeping a band like ours together is hard work. We're far different from a jobbing band, where subs are always available to seamlessly step in and fill an empty spot. In those situations everyone plays from behind music stands and wears formal attire, so if the faces change from gig to gig it's hardly noticeable. The musicians have been trained to read music, which makes it sound as if they've played with this same group of people for years. Rock-and-roll bands that play bars and festivals don't use music stands, so whatever musical arrangements you work out to segue from one song to another must be committed to memory. It's practically impossible to work subs into this scenario unless they learn all the material by heart. There's also another possibility, which involves hiring a chart writer to put all the music down on paper, but that would cost a fortune. Identifying and training new players requires patience, especially when it comes to giving that person the necessary time to learn the band's repertoire. Having gigs already on the calendar can ensure that all this gets done in a timely fashion, but it can also add pressure. At least I know our bass player will be there for us until we break in someone new.

Day 20 *FEBRUARY 12*

PREDICTIONS
- *Meet with accountant to prepare tax return*
- *Finalize keyboard player auditions*

DIARY
Today I meet with our new accountant to prepare our tax return for last year. Our band's lead guitar player has recommended this woman, who has done his return and those of his friends and family for a number of years. She also has a great deal of experience working with musicians and other self-employed types who receive multiple 1099s and have complex filings. My W2 and all my 1099s, plus bank statements and the accumulated paperwork from our personal stocks and investments, make up the largest pile. Next comes the form that shows the income I paid out as a bandleader, plus all my business expenses. I've been very thorough in my bookkeeping, which makes her job easier. Our meeting lasts around ninety minutes, and I leave there feeling she did everything possible to dig up the maximum number of legal deductions for me. I'll be receiving a rather hefty refund on my Federal filing. However, some of that money will be paid to the state of Illinois since I owe them several hundred dollars. Best of all, I'm finally showing a substantial income as a professional musician. For a long time my expenses as a singer have exceeded my earnings, and it's a great feeling to know that all those years of hard work are finally paying off. I'm happy about working with this

accountant and I'm sure we'll use her services again next year.

Over the past few days I've been playing traffic cop, sorting out e-mail correspondence from my band mates as well as the two keyboard players we hope to audition. It seems like a nearly impossible task. Just when it looks like we're all set to agree on a time and date, there's always one person with a conflict. The player who was worried about playing full-time informs me that his recurring back injury has caused his doctor to caution him against playing for the next four to six weeks. That leaves us with only one keyboardist to check out for now, and I see he's offered us the choice of several audition slots that should work with the rest of our schedules. We tentatively settle on next Monday evening, which I expect will allow him enough time to prepare the songs we've selected to play together. I also send a reply to the injured player, wishing him well and telling him I'll keep his information on file should there be a time we need to find a new or additional keyboard player.

Next I notify our band members that we'll get together Monday at seven o'clock to prepare for the audition. I'd like us to sound as tight as possible before the keyboard player shows up at 8:15 P.M. With all the bands out there to choose from, it's important that we put our best musical face forward. I'm sure the top players audition for more than one band at a time, looking for the best possible fit. We want to make a positive impression on a new player, and we also hope to reach like-minded thinking as far as the frequency of gigs we perform, how much each of us earns, and which personality traits go best together. While I realize most of these elements are beyond my control, the part about playing well is completely within our grasp.

I've been sent another new song to record, and I believe I'll lay down the tracks at our bass player's place rather than with our lead guitarist. My regular collaborator is booked up this week with voiceover work, and I'm hoping I can cajole our bass player back into a full-time band commitment. Also, our bass player owns different equipment and employs different recording techniques, so I'd like to hear how these raw tracks sound when coming out of a different studio. If there's one drawback to this plan, it's that our bass player's place is an hour from home while the other one is a mere fifteen minutes away. Knowing that the Web site's tracks should be turned around in three to four business days, I leave our bass player a voice-mail message to ask about this week's availability of his recording studio. In the past he's offered to record me for free whenever he's not otherwise booked.

LESSONS/PROBLEMS
Juggling everyone's schedules is a tricky and exhausting task. My band mates have priorities that are important to them, even if I don't see it. I need to respect their choices and do my best to accommodate those situations. Sometimes it seems like I'm sacrificing my own priorities more than others, but that comes with the territory of being the person in charge. The more often we play, the more money we all make. Since I earn the most, I suppose I must sacrifice the most as well.

A VIEW FROM INSIDE THE VOCAL RECORDING BOOTH AT JOHN'S STUDIO.

Day 21 *FEBRUARY 13*

PREDICTIONS
- *Compose sample voiceover spots*
- *Record one or more voiceover demos*

DIARY

It's time to finish writing those voiceover spots, which are comprised of a few sentences about different businesses or products. I'll need a dozen or so that can be delivered with different intonations and voice inflections. Once we're finished recording we'll pick out some music to play in the background, although that will probably have to wait for another day. Many voiceover artists perform specialty voices such as children, cartoon characters or imitations of celebrities, but I'll leave that to the professionals and accept

RECORDING VOICE-OVER SPOTS AT JOHN'S.

my limitations in this field. I'm interested in creating a demo disk that will contain various samples of commercial tag lines, or perhaps even on-hold messages, and try to tap into that line of work. Some of my spots are fanciful, while others come directly from actual radio commercials. The average listener is exposed to hundreds of radio voiceovers daily, promoting every kind of product under the sun—including the radio stations themselves. I also do some Internet surfing and listen to voiceover demos that are posted on line. I listen to six or seven different people to get an idea of the variety of spots they have, and also to borrow the gist of some of the spots. I don't copy them down verbatim, but they give me ideas for the kinds of spots I want to write.

There are some great artists out there, people blessed with interesting sounding voices who use them in fascinating ways. This is a serious field for actors, where many of them make a substantial living. I'm just hoping to find a local business or two that likes the sound of my speaking voice and wants to hire me to record their on-hold messages, and perhaps do some industrial work for them.

Here's a sample of one of my voiceover spots:
"Griffin Audio Media—for all your recording needs. Our knowledgeable staff can assist you in all of your various studio projects. For a full listing of our services, be sure to check out our Web site at griffin-audio-media-dot-com. Griffin Audio Media, a favorite of recording professionals everywhere."

And one more:
"Uh oh, guys. It's Valentine's Day, and you've blown it already? Want a sure-fire way to win back her heart? Think Kaye's, the perfect place to find the perfect diamond for your special someone. Remember, every kiss begins with Kaye's."

I head over to the recording studio with my notes in hand. My lead guitar player records a lot of voiceover work, including commercials, technical readings, on-hold messages, and industrial material. He checks over my scripts and says they sound legitimate, so we begin to record them. I'm told the busiest voiceover artists are those who sound warm, bright, and sunny. It's interesting how the same sentence sounds different if I'm smiling. You can actually hear the happiness in someone's voice, which makes the material more enticing. Whether it's promoting a product or reciting an on-hold message, businesses want their voiceovers to sound friendly and inviting. I'm sure there are many studies that have shown a direct link between improved sales and the customer's positive reaction to commercials that promote a product, service, or business.

We record each spot two or three times to guarantee that my diction is clear without being over-enunciated. We also listen for my delivery of the lines, making sure that each take sounds both friendly and professional. This is all new to me and very different from a singing performance. Before today I never thought so much about speaking and how each word sounds as it comes out of my mouth.

LESSONS/PROBLEMS
Recording voiceover spots is a challenge, and it shouldn't be viewed as an easy way to supplement your income. It's a highly competitive field that's filled primarily with actors. I'm hopeful that someone will be attracted to the natural sound of my voice, as there's not a whole lot I can do to change it. Some people happen to be blessed with an interesting or a commanding sound, but not everyone is James Earl Jones. Nonetheless, there is work out there for a more average-sounding voice, so long as it comes across as warm and friendly. The things I can work on involve diction and the clear delivery of copy.

THE MARYANN AND THE PROFESSORS MAGNET FROM OUR PROMOTIONAL MATERIALS.

Day 22 *FEBRUARY 16*

PREDICTIONS
- *Participate in a recording session*
- *Ship out promo kits to private clubs*

DIARY

I'm off to my bass player's studio to record a song for my Internet client. This is the first song they've sent me that I actually like. It has a catchy melody and the lyrics are rather poignant. The song also feels right for my range and timbre. On my way over I listen to the song on the CD I burned, both the version with the guide vocals as well as those with only the orchestral track. I'd already e-mailed the songs to my colleague, so he should be all set to record it. Because of conflicting schedules, we have only about an hour to record

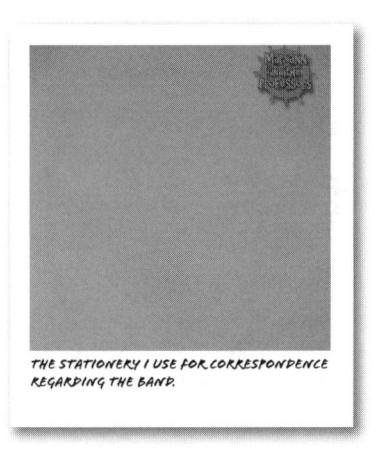

THE STATIONERY I USE FOR CORRESPONDENCE
REGARDING THE BAND.

the main vocal line and several lines of harmony. I was hoping to get there sooner to get a shot at re-recording a song I'd done a few weeks ago. When I checked to see why I hadn't yet been paid for the job, the client reported some dissatisfaction with my performance and asked that it be redone. One drawback of remote recording involves running the risk that the vocals won't be exactly what the songwriter or producer wants. The woman who runs this particular site reports that the composer felt I could turn in a more vibrant performance, based upon the two or three pieces I'd sung for him earlier. I'll perform the new song first, and then we'll check the time.

As I feared, we use up the entire hour for the new song and its harmony tracks. I decide to provide two versions of the lead track. The first one is a note-for-note and second-by-second match to the vocal line that appears on the

TESTING A MIC AT AN OPEN STUDIO SESSION.

songwriter's scratch track. The other version is the sort of performance I think he'd want if he were the singer. There are several places in the song where it feels natural to hold the notes longer than written, as well as other spots where the cadence of the phrases sound better when I alter them just a bit. My recording engineer agrees with my reading. Since he works full-time as a music producer, I feel good about offering the client an alternative. As far as redoing the other song, I'll need to check everyone's schedule to see when we can get it done. Before leaving we chat a bit regarding Monday's audition, and I also make sure he knows that the door is always open for him to return to us as a regular player.

Reaching home at three o'clock, I now have time to assemble some promotional kits. I want to ship them out to places I've played with my jobbing orchestra. When each venue's party planner sees that I'm the one submitting the material, I'm hoping they'll listen to the enclosed CD and consider hiring my band at some later date. I have no idea how many unsolicited kits they might receive by mail, and I'm not sure if they have a system in place where certain vendors provide a finder's fee. I see that in other businesses, so why should this be any different? I have no problem paying someone a commission if they refer a client to us and we get the job, which is no different than offering an agent a percentage of the gross for their effort.

Off the top of my head I come up with half a dozen places my jobbing orchestra has played over the years. I pull contact information off the Internet and compose a cover letter that mentions my jobbing orchestra as a reference and then introduces my other band that may be appropriate for their smaller functions. Then I include the usual blather—a short paragraph that describes our start under corporate sponsorship, followed by how the band expanded its repertoire to serve private functions that required a party band to keep people dancing all night long, and so on. These six letters are stuffed into envelopes along with song lists, pictures of the band, testimonials, a list of former clients, biographies of each band member, a logo magnet, a demo CD, and finally my business card.

LESSONS/PROBLEMS
This business of remote recording can be tricky. If the songwriter fails to provide details as to how the song should be performed, it's up to the singer to offer the best possible

interpretation. I try to hit every note they write, and with the same timing. In the past, I've been instructed to not vary the melody at all, and to sing it exactly as it's presented on the scratch track. This is the first time I've had someone ask me to redo something—which is fine—but I wish I knew from the beginning what kind of sound they had in mind. I hate the idea of re-recording it without a clearer message, especially when I'm relying on friends to give me free studio time.

A PROGRAM FROM THE SINGER'S SHOWCASE.

Day 23 FEBRUARY 18

PREDICTIONS
- Contact the participants in February's showcase
- Work on the showcase program

DIARY
Today I expect to receive song selections and biographical data from the four singers who will participate in the upcoming showcase. I usually have to chase down one or two singers to get this information, and there have been times where I had to mark "not available at press time" in the program. To avoid duplication, it's vital that I know which songs everyone plans to sing. That information also helps me determine their order of performance. In checking my e-mail inbox today, I see that three out of the four have

complied with my request. The fourth singer, a seasoned pro, is the woman I tabbed to replace the one who was forced to drop out. I can always pull an old bio from an earlier show, so I send her a quick reminder to let me know her song choices. If she wants to sing something already on the program, I'll give her a call. I know she has no shortage of songs in her repertoire.

I keep the program template stored on my home computer. The information includes the names of the four singers, biographical sketches, a list of songs to be presented, and the names of everyone who makes up the evening's house band. The front cover includes the showcase logo, the date of the performance, and a list of the singers' names. The back cover posts dates and locations of upcoming showcases, how to reach us for consideration in future showcases, and details on junior showcases that feature singers under the age of eighteen. The front and back covers require a minimum of editing, while the inside pages must be changed completely. The greatest effort goes into biographical editing, since they're much too long to fit in the allotted space. Due to legibility issues, I'm not comfortable using anything smaller than a nine-point font. As I review bios, I'm often struck by how the best singers generally come across as the most humble. Everyone wants to appear as accomplished as possible, but I think it's best to let one's singing do the talking. Two of the bios I've received are for singers new to the scene, and they've both gone a bit overboard. Not only is there not enough room for all the copy they wrote, but they also read like they've been excessively padded. I'll contact them for a rewrite, or I'll edit them on my own.

With the show ten days away, I'll send out an e-mail notice even if I've received the person's details. I use it to remind them of the order in which singers will rehearse, along with what time to report. I also prompt everyone to bring along as many of their friends as possible, since a broad show of support helps all the singers. Finally, I give them my contact information once again, asking them to give me a call if they need anything before the show date. I'll follow up in a week to check in, answer any last-minute questions, and assure them we'll be putting on a terrific show. Any opportunity I can take to boost their confidence is time well spent.

LESSONS/PROBLEMS

Handling younger singers can be a challenge. I don't want them to think I don't believe in their talent and potential, but I also don't want them to overextend themselves or look foolish on the stage. Part of my job as producer is to keep everyone focused and make sure we put on a great show. The best way to handle ego issues is to speak plainly. I tell singers not to inflate their biographies, since most people won't remember any of it. What they will remember is the performance—if it was great, or if it was painful. It's vital for performers to focus on their singing rather than advance promotion. As the host, I open each set and sing the last song of the night. Consequently I must choose my songs wisely, finding material that complements what everyone else is singing. Our primary goal involves increasing the number of people who attend our showcases, no matter who is on the program. We're selling a concept at the same time we're promoting local singers and ourselves as the producers.

Day 24 FEBRUARY 19

PREDICTIONS
- *Audition a new keyboard player*

DIARY
Our bass player composed an e-mail message to me at two o'clock this morning, telling me he's unable to attend our audition session this evening. No explanation accompanies his message, other than that one sentence and the word "sorry." After reading his note, I'm furious. How can we audition a new player without the bass player? I call his home and cell phone numbers, ending up with his voice-mail greeting. I leave him the same message at both locations, essentially saying that he can't do this to us, especially after promising to not leave us high and dry until we found an adequate replacement. I also remind him that I confirmed the date and time with him three times via e-mail, plus the other day when I participated in a recording session at his home studio.

I call my lead guitarist for some advice. I'm not interested in postponing an audition that took so much effort to schedule, especially since I have the impression the keyboardist was getting frustrated by all the back-and forth wrangling we did among ourselves. I certainly don't want to turn him off from the band before he's even had a chance to play with us. I also call our regular keyboard player, asking him to prep the audition songs on his keyboard bass, if that's possible. However, this process essentially defeats the purpose of hiring a second player, since we're anxious to hear how two keyboards will work together on a lot of songs, and also how two guitars plus one keyboard would work on others. If our regular keyboardist is forced to play the bass line on his piano, we won't get to hear any of this.

As usual, my lead guitarist succeeds in calming me down by putting things in the most straightforward of terms. We'll run the audition without our bass player, which still gives us the means to gauge the guy's level of play and how well he might fit in with the group. One thing is clear—we need to start our search for a new bass player immediately. We discuss the positive elements of finding a new player— someone far more reliable, not only punctual for gigs and rehearsals, but better at learning the material correctly and in a timely manner. Our bass player is capable of faking his way through songs, but the songs lack the necessary "punch" because he never takes the time to learn the proper bass lines.

Once the audition is finished, I'm glad we followed through with it. As a bonus, this guy has spent his last four years as a bass player in a cover band. We explained that our regular bass player had an emergency and we didn't want to postpone the audition, which is why we continued without him. He played keyboard on several songs we'd provided as audition tunes, played rhythm guitar on a few others, and even picked up the bass on one we hadn't prepared. His guitar playing was acceptable, and he did a pretty good job picking out harmonies while singing backup. His lead vocals were probably his weakest element, but I guess he'll do fine if we're careful as to which songs he sings. His bass playing was exceptional, and our drummer loved playing with him. He has a really great personality and looks to be a total team player, willing to play and do whatever is necessary to make our band sound its best. As he packed up his gear, he told me he has one more audition to make plus a callback with another band. Both of these auditions are later in the week, so we agree to follow up after they're finished and see how everyone feels about proceeding. After he leaves, the four of us discuss what we heard. We agree that I should ask him to join the band when I call him on Thursday. If he turns us down, we'll go back to the ad boards and start the process all over again. We have to do that for a bass player as well, and I'll post that ad tomorrow.

LESSONS/PROBLEMS

The prospect of replacing a long-time band member can be depressing. However, I'm lucky to have someone else in our group who can help me see the proper perspective. It's daunting to break in a new player, especially since we really can't begin to tackle new material until they learn all the old stuff. But on the plus side, if the new player already knows songs we'd like to add to our repertoire, that will encourage us to expand what we play. Furthermore, a new player may have connections to clubs where we'd like to play but haven't, plus existing relationships with agents who don't currently book us.

MY FIRST WHITE SOX ANTHEM.

Day 25 *FEBRUARY 22*

PREDICTIONS
- *Call our prospective keyboard player*
- *Respond to bass player ads*

DIARY
I begin my day by resolving to read every bass player ad that's posted on my two favorite musician-wanted job boards, and to respond to whoever answered the ad I placed two days ago on Craig's List. The first thing I notice is that there are tons of bands looking for bass players. You might say it's a seller's market, where it's more like the band is auditioning for the player instead of the other way around. It takes me more than an hour to read through all the posts,

although I find only five ads worthy of a response. The factors in my decision-making include the type of music they want to play and their experience. My message to each of the five is brief. I begin by asking how they feel about playing in a cover band that does clubs and corporate gigs, and whether they're comfortable with rehearsing on our side of town. I want them to know this up front, in case our rehearsal spot is too much of a commute for them. I've received a few responses to my posted ad, with most people asking the name of our band, which places and how often we play, and where we rehearse. I provide everyone our URL, since our Web site gives the sort of information they'll need to decide whether or not to proceed with us.

The jobbing orchestra where I'm the lead singer has sent me their advance list of dates for this year, including some holds. This latter item is where we "hold" a date for a client. If we get approached to perform elsewhere on that day, we'll check back with the first party to confirm their interest in hiring us for their event. The list includes only thirty solid dates so far. The orchestra is likely to pick up another six to ten dates throughout the year, but these numbers have been falling year after year. Most jobbing orchestras I know have struggled since 2000, except for the well-known groups. My orchestra has managed to maintain a steady supply of gigs, mostly due to our bandleader's reputation and his eclectic taste in music. But starting three years ago, even his numbers began to slip. I try to pick up more work for my band and as a sub in other jobbing orchestras to compensate for the lost income, but that's tough. Having live music at a celebration can be costly compared to just playing an iPod or spinning CDs. Disc jockeys have seriously cut into the live music business, even though there are some who charge more than a live band because of their popularity. The general state of our economy directly affects this business. Anyone who throws a party has to contend with the rising costs of food, liquor, music, flowers, photography, video, party favors, centerpieces, and invitations. When it comes to cutting corners, the choice between a band and recorded music is often the first decision they make. Even if the client decides on live music, invariably they'll hire the smallest ensemble possible that will also get their guests up and dancing.

The keyboard player we auditioned Monday was unavailable by phone, so I leave him a message to call me at his earliest convenience.

LESSONS/PROBLEMS
Maintaining steady work is becoming more of a challenge with each passing year. Since the number of my orchestra gigs has declined, I'm trying to make up the difference with band gigs. That's actually better for me financially, since I bring home more as the leader of our band than I do as a lead singer in someone else's orchestra. However, our band is so new to the market that it will take years before we ever get the same number of gigs my jobbing orchestra currently plays. It took nearly six years for our band to hit the fifty-gig-a-year mark, and we've pretty much stagnated there over the past half-dozen years. With the current state of live music

I have no way of knowing if our band will ever double those numbers, as long as the economy remains in its current funk.

STUDIO WHERE THE VOICE OVER SPOTS WERE RECORDED.

Day 26 *FEBRUARY 23*

PREDICTIONS
- *Select music for my voiceover demo*
- *Check for responses from potential bass players and keyboardists*

DIARY

I have responses from two bass players who want to set up auditions with us. Both of them visited our Web site and liked what they saw and heard. Both also state they have a lot of experience with gigs, but I'm cautious about that claim. Some players think "a lot of experience" means one or two gigs a month over the course of a couple of years. I'm inclined to define it as having three hundred-plus shows under their belts. I believe I'll wait to hear from a few more

THE MIXING BOARD IN THE STUDIO.

players before I commit to scheduling auditions.

While I'm checking my e-mail, the keyboard player we'd auditioned calls me back. We make small talk for a minute or two and then I tell him everyone in the band agreed that he was our top choice to join us. He's pleased with the way everything went during the audition and agrees to come on board. I'm glad to hear that he liked us as much as we liked him, although I'm sorry his audition didn't include a bass player. At first I'm inclined not to tell him that we're losing our bass player, since he made it clear he wants to join a working band, not a start-up. Of course, there's still a part of me that hopes our bass player will change his mind, which means I wouldn't have to divulge that information. We chat at length about his former bands and the kind of music they performed. I explain how our band has evolved over the years and offer to e-mail him a list of our confirmed and held

A VOCAL TRACK ON THE COMPUTER SHOWING THE TONES AS WAVE LENGTHS.

dates, along with our song list. We also discuss rehearsal times and what might work best for him, and I mention we often rotate from one band member's house to another to ease the driving burden. He doesn't mind the commute since he can't offer us rehearsal space in his home. After spending all this time on the phone, I decide it's best to broach the subject of needing a new bass player. Since some of those reasons are personal, I don't disclose exactly why our bass player may need a break, but I feel better knowing that I leveled with him about what's going on with the band. We agree to confirm some rehearsal dates via e-mail, and he'll look over our song list to let me know which ones he'll need to learn. I'll send him those songs on a CD or two, along with whatever charts I might have.

I e-mail everyone the good news about our new keyboard player before heading out the door to finish my voiceover demo. Over the years, my lead guitarist has accumulated several CDs filled with snippets of music specifically designed to serve as background material for commercials and industrial videos. We look at each script I recorded and discuss what sort of music would work best in the background. This process is new to me, and I have no idea how one goes about picking out a piece of music, especially when there are so many clips to choose from. Thankfully I'm in the presence of an expert, so I defer to his choices. We listen to each one of the spots while he runs several different selections behind them. Before long I start to hear how different background music affects the overall impression a commercial can have, even though the script is the same. Depending on the subject and the voice inflections I've used, certain clips fit perfectly while others sound terribly out of place. One of my samples is an "on-hold" spot, so we seek out smooth, mellow music to play behind it—the sort of thing you'd expect to hear in a doctor's waiting room. For the jewelry spot, something romantic seems best. Because of all the steps we needed to take—listening to sample clips, trying different pieces behind the same text, and deciding on the best background music for each commercial—we only have time to finish about half a dozen spots.

LESSONS/PROBLEMS
With bands as with life, honesty is always the best policy. I feel much better having told our new keyboard player about our bass player's impending departure. Had I kept that news from him, he may have lost his trust in the band and changed his mind about joining us. With that settled, I was in a better frame of mind when it came time to dress

up my voiceovers. I was amazed by how much I didn't know about the process. Creating the copy, finding the right voice to speak the lines with just the right delivery, selecting the background music, and adding sound effects—it's much more work than most people realize. Going through this process made me appreciate the talent that goes into making those fifteen- and thirty-second radio spots that people take for granted.

Day 27 ~~FEBRUARY 28~~

PREDICTIONS
- *Rehearse and host the singers' showcase*

DIARY
I've heard from two more players interested in trying out for our bass guitar position—a guy in his mid-40s and a girl in her early 30s. Both claim experience in singing backups and harmonies. I'm actually far more interested in the woman, due to her voice range. Our keyboard player tends to sing a lot in his falsetto voice. If our band included a woman to sing the higher-placed notes, our primary keyboardist could revert to his lower, more comfortable register. Now that we have four people prepared to audition, it will be a challenge to get everything organized. It's not just the playing time to consider, but also the added effort in setting up and breaking down our gear. It's good for people to see that they have some competition, so I don't mind if one player arrives while we're finishing up with an earlier one. I send out e-mails to each of the four bassists, suggesting two possible audition days and times, and then I e-mail my band mates to let them know we'll plan on auditioning both days since we now have four people to hear.

Then it's time to rehearse tonight's showcase. I'm pleased to see that everyone in the band has arrived, and it's equally important that each of the four singers gets here on time to make their rehearsal slot. I can't go over my songs until everyone else is finished, and it's not very professional if I'm rehearsing while the audience is filing in. Our first singer is prompt and her practice goes well. She's done these showcases before and is familiar with the drill. Three of her four songs are fairly common jobbing tunes, so the band already knows them. This is the woman I brought in as a last-minute replacement. She's a pro and has worked with this band a number of times in the past. I'm hopeful she'll attract a crowd, although she's had the least amount of time to promote her appearance. A while back, our executive producer decided that each singer had to guarantee a minimum of ten paying audience members. Prospective showcase singers are told this up front, so it's no surprise when the night of the performance rolls around. If they feel they can't attract that many people, they can either hold off until they can meet their quota or else be willing to pay the difference out of their own pocket.

Our second singer is also on time, and she asks me to sing backup on two of her pieces. That's part of my job as the host, which involves helping out our performers any way I can. Her set sounds good. As we're wrapping up her last song in the set, I notice that singer number four has just arrived. Because time is short, I have her begin rehearsing in place of our third singer, a young woman who has never performed with a live band. Then my cell phone rings, and it's our missing singer. She appears to be lost, but I calm her down while explaining that I'll do my rehearsing while we wait for her to arrive. I'm busy taking dinner orders from the band when she walks in the door, and I rush her onto the

HOSTING AND PERFORMING AT A SHOWCASE.

stage. She's decided to change one of her selections since we last spoke. That means I'll have to make a change as well, since I'd planned to cover a similar piece by the same performer to open the evening.

In general, the show goes quite well. Our last-minute addition brings in a dozen people, and the woman who closes the show brought in twice that many. The evening's biggest disappointment was the novice. We count on untried singers to bring in tons of people, since they usually have friends who want to see them perform for the very first time. This singer brought only her mother, and our executive producer was fairly unhappy about it. Once her set was over—she was the first scheduled singer on tonight's program—we knew that anyone else who walked in the door was there to see someone else. Additionally, the folks collecting cover charges are instructed to ask patrons if they've come to see a particular singer or if they simply dropped in to see the show. During intermission, the executive producer pulls this new singer aside and reminds her of the agreement to bring in at least ten people or pay the equivalent cover. We try to pay the musicians at least $100 apiece, which means we need fifty audience members simply to break even. When every singer can bring in ten people, most of our expenses are met. Later the executive producer tells me she'll place our novice singer's name on the "do not re-book" list.

LESSONS/PROBLEMS

Producing a show takes organizational skills, plus the ability to crack the whip whenever necessary. With rehearsal time so limited, we can't spend too much time on any one song. Each performer is allotted a total of twenty-five minutes, and it's usually a struggle to perform each number more than once or twice in that span. Oftentimes I'll need to change my own songs at the drop of a hat and learn backup harmonies in an instant. It can be a challenge to pull off a good show, but the rewards are great when it's obvious that the crowd has enjoyed itself.

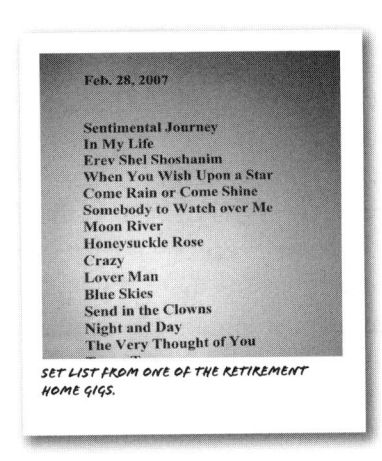

> Feb. 28, 2007
>
> Sentimental Journey
> In My Life
> Erev Shel Shoshanim
> When You Wish Upon a Star
> Come Rain or Come Shine
> Somebody to Watch over Me
> Moon River
> Honeysuckle Rose
> Crazy
> Lover Man
> Blue Skies
> Send in the Clowns
> Night and Day
> The Very Thought of You

SET LIST FROM ONE OF THE RETIREMENT HOME GIGS.

Day 28 MARCH 1

PREDICTIONS
- Confirm bass player auditions
- Perform a set at a retirement home

DIARY
Tonight is my second "old folks" gig at the retirement home. My piano player is an old hand at jobbing and reads charts with the best of them. Before I leave home I'll need to make up a set list and log onto the Internet to dig up some interesting tidbits, which I'll use to introduce each of the songs I'm singing. The last time I was here, several of the residents told me another singer performed the exact same show, song for song and in the exact same order, during two consecutive visits a month apart. I was amazed that

they remembered the program from one month to the next. But with that warning in mind, I'm careful to select fifteen different songs for tonight.

Before diving into that task, it's important that I finalize the audition schedule for our prospective bass players. Two are set for our first evening, but I'm still waiting to hear back from the others. For the two who have already confirmed their auditions, I send them the list of songs we'll play. This selection took some serious thought and a fair amount of conference time with my band mates. We play a fairly diverse repertoire, so it's important to find someone capable of playing all these styles. Our ideal player will have a firm grasp on timing and should be able to match up well with our drummer, since together they're responsible for keeping the beat and driving the songs forward. If the drummer doesn't feel he can lock up with the bass player, then we'll need to keep looking. It's the same for two vocalists, who may sing great solo but whose voices don't blend well. Since our drummer's opinion is most important in this process, I consulted him first. We made sure that the list includes a wide variety of music, including several different rock genres plus Motown, disco, swing, and a ballad.

Thinking about that list reminds me of the one I need to create for this evening's performance. I'm careful to choose songs different from my last show, placing them in an order that offers a variety of moods. With just a singer and a piano player, it can be difficult for one song to sound different from the next if they're all the same style. I decide to open

AN INVOICE FOR THE RETIREMENT HOME GIG.

with a medium-tempo standard, followed by a Beatles ballad, then an Israeli love song sung in Hebrew, followed by a swinger, another ballad, a waltz, and so on.

The show goes well, and I'm pleased they're a fairly attentive audience. The songs are well received and, just like last time, many of the residents are very complimentary. A few go out of their way to tell me stories about what some of the songs meant to them. There's a Hebrew word, "mitzvah," which means "good deed." The pianist and I look upon these kinds of gigs as mitzvahs, since the money tends to be on the low side. Of course, it's unlikely that we'd find a high-paying job on a Thursday night, and we're only on stage for an hour, but we know these songs bring the seniors joy and pleasant memories. As a result, we feel good about what we're doing no matter what the pay might be.

LESSONS/PROBLEMS

When the band auditions for a new member, it's the entire group that's making the decision. I'm sure to include my band mates when it comes to interviewing prospects as well as choosing the audition songs. Everyone has their own idea as to what they want to hear. In the case of a bass player, the drummer is most interested in the timing and how they can sync up, the lead guitarist wants to know if they're capable of strong support without overplaying, and I want to hear their timing and judge their ability to provide backup vocals. As long as everyone feels they're an important part of the process, we should be able to come to a unanimous decision once all the players have performed.

Day 29 MARCH 3

PREDICTIONS
- Sing at an afternoon bar mitzvah gig
- Sing some more at an evening wedding gig

DIARY
Today is expected to be an exhausting one since I'm doing a double—two performances in one day—including an afternoon bar mitzvah party out in the suburbs and an evening gig downtown. I have these every now and again, although they're much more common during the summer. My morning begins by firing up the computer and checking my e-mail inbox. I've received confirmation from all four bass players regarding their audition times, so I write to my band mates and let them know we're on schedule as planned.

I'll bring along two changes of clothes, as I'll run from one gig to the other. Since they're both a long way from my house, it hardly makes sense to return home and change. My afternoon gig is a bar mitzvah and I usually dress a bit low-key for those, meaning black slacks and a matching top plus black loafers. For evening gigs, especially ones we do downtown, my typical outfit is much more formal. Tonight I'll wear a long black dress, stockings, and dressy shoes with a medium heel. I also pack my makeup bag so I can touch up between gigs.

The bar mitzvah goes smoothly, and I'm pleased to see lots of familiar faces in the crowd since we play regularly for members of this congregation. While I'm taking a break between sets, a couple stops by to tell me they're enjoying themselves but need to depart and prepare for their son's bar mitzvah this evening. Then they mention looking forward to my singing later on. Naturally I ask if their festivities are scheduled for downtown, but instead they name a popular hotel out near O'Hare Airport. I reply by explaining that I'm singing downtown, at which point their faces show confusion before confronting my bandleader to ask why I'm not scheduled to perform at their party. Only after I finish my next set does the bandleader explain that he's triple-booked today, including this afternoon gig, the suburban job this evening with some other singer, and the gig I'm singing downtown. I apologize to him for causing any problem with his clients, but I truly had no idea what his plans were for the evening. He tells me not to worry about it as we pack things up here, explaining that we'll discuss the situation later at the downtown venue.

My downtown gig is a wedding at a members-only club. The bride and groom are older—late 40s to early 50s—and this is a second marriage for both. When the bandleader arrives, everything becomes clearer in my mind. As I surmised, he booked another singer for the airport-area bar mitzvah, knowing that I was already committed to the wedding downtown. However, the folks putting on the party have heard me sing a number of times before and are anxious for me to put in an appearance at their party. The

SINGING WITH THE JOBBING ORCHESTRA.

bandleader asks if I'm willing to head for the airport hotel close to the end of this gig so I can at least provide an hour's worth of music up there. Since he's planning to do the same, I sign on as well. The guitar player on the downtown bandstand is a good singer. If this party happens to go into overtime, he's more than capable of stepping in once I leave. As luck would have it, the gig does not run late, possibly because the bridal party and their guests are a bit older. The party winds down around ten o'clock, after a 6:30 P.M. start time, and the bandleader and I discreetly depart. We arrive at the Marriott with the bar mitzvah reception in full swing. Walking in I'm practically hijacked by the conga line that's snaking around the perimeter of the room, and the parents of the bar mitzvah boy wave hello as I head for the raised bandstand. It's great fun to join a musical number already in progress, as well as a pleasure to share the stage with the woman who's singing tonight. She's very talented, a bit older than me, and one of the people in the region I truly admire. We have a blast sharing the spotlight, and the guests clearly enjoy themselves as the party goes into overtime. We finally manage to shut things down at 11:30 P.M., and I head for home knowing I've earned a substantial paycheck for a full day's work.

LESSONS/PROBLEMS
When I first realized I would have to sing at three parties today to keep my bandleader out of hot water with his client, I was apprehensive and even a bit annoyed. After doing two full gigs on no more than five hours of sleep the night before, all I could think about was crashing at home. However, when I realized the family really wanted to see me at their son's bar mitzvah, I couldn't deny them. Things turned out much better than I expected. I got my second wind as the energy in the room swept over me, and the chance to share some songs with a vocalist I respected was merely the icing on the cake.

Day 30 *MARCH 8*

PREDICTIONS
- *Make follow-up calls on promo kits*
- *Audition two bass players*

DIARY
Over the past eight weeks I've mailed out a couple of dozen promo kits, and in today's e-mail inbox I receive two responses. These kits were sent to various catering managers, club directors, and events planners around town, pretty much on a cold-call basis. Under those circumstances I really didn't expect them to acknowledge receiving the package, especially since they're up to their ears in marketing materials from numerous vendors. All sorts of suppliers want to find a way onto a recommended vendor list, including florists, photographers and those dreaded DJs. As a result, the responses I receive today are a pleasant surprise. One comes from the department manager at a country club we've played before, and the other was sent by an event planner I worked with through one of my jobbing orchestra gigs. The banquet manager thanks me for sending the materials, mentioning that she recalls our band from a private party we played there last winter. She promises to add us to their list of vendors and will let me know if something arises. That's all I really ask for in these situations. Should we get hired there in the future, I'll know it was because the client got the promo CD from the club and enjoyed it. The message from the event planner is just

as positive. Recommendations by busy party planners can make a huge difference in the number of jobs a band lands. First, a client will hire us based solely on the planner's advice. Assuming we come through with a great performance, the event coordinator would have no hesitation in suggesting us again and again to her clients.

I spend the next hour calling everyone else from my marketing list to see if they received our information and what they thought of our CD. As expected, I end up leaving quite a few messages because the contact person is either on another call, in a meeting, or out of the office. I manage to speak with half a dozen people, all of whom have similar questions for me—how many pieces we have in the band, whether we travel with our own sound system, what is our experience in playing various types of functions, and if we have a Web site. Several people ask for referrals and our basic price structure that can be passed along to their clients or club members. Because a few of these people know me from my jobbing orchestra gigs, they want to know if our band is booked out of that office. In the Chicago area it's not uncommon for smaller bands to book gigs through a larger band's office, with the bandleader of the larger band acting in the dual role of agent. If someone calls to book the larger band and they're already committed on that date, the bandleader will suggests the smaller band as a substitute. This process can broaden the smaller band's reputation, because they get a chance to work for a client who may not know of them. I tried this once with my jobbing orchestra, but I was less than pleased with our cut so I decided not to do it again.

After dinner at home with my family, it's time to audition two of our prospective bass players. The first one on the schedule is the only female of the four. Not only does she fail to show, but she never even calls. I'm highly disappointed whenever anyone does that to us, but this was an especially painful jab. I was looking forward to hearing her play and sing, but I also feel this sort of behavior hurts a woman's chances of gaining the respect she deserves in a male-dominated field. We kill some time by playing around with a few new song ideas, and the second player shows up right on time. As he sets up we make small talk, asking about past band experiences, what sort of music he prefers to play, and so on. He's curious about what happened to our other bass player, and I reply that he simply needed a break. We play about a dozen songs, with him singing lead on two and trying to sing backup on two others. He brought three different bass guitars along—a four-string, a five-string, and even a six-string! He's a very good player but not much of a singer. We let him know that we're auditioning two other people next week and will be in touch after that.

LESSONS/PROBLEMS
Making follow-up marketing calls is a tedious process, and I always feel a bit vulnerable since I'm opening myself up for rejection. It's important to know that the material has arrived in the proper hands. However, if they liked what they saw and heard, it's my opinion that they'd contact us—as did those two people today. The reality of the situation is that

most people are too busy with other tasks, so a quick call to remind them of our existence may lead to a booking, and hopefully not being blackballed because the planner felt I pestered them. As with the earlier keyboard auditions, our effort to hire a new bass player will be tedious. Adding talent to an existing band is a balancing act, where you look for complementary personalities as well as matching skill levels. I need to keep an open mind and also rely on the advice of my colleagues.

EPILOGUE

Quite a few things have happened to the band and my solo career since this diary was composed. I sang our national anthem at a White Sox baseball game in May, and my family plus our lead guitarist were part of the crowd. I discovered that the team hires local bands to play outside two of the ticket gates prior to game time. Although they were booked solid for the rest of the season, the marketing department promised to consider us for next year. My piano player and I picked up several more gigs at assisted-living facilities. These jobs involve decent pay and almost no stress, plus we have the satisfaction of making elderly people really happy for an hour a month. The session allows them to forget their aches and pains for a short time and enjoy the memories the music brings back to them. It's like playing for your grandparents and their friends, and it feels good to do something with the talent we have.

I picked up several more remote recording gigs off the Web site where I'm listed. For a local musician I sang backup vocals on a fourteen-track children's record. The process comprised six sessions spread out over several months because of ongoing conflicts among the artist, the recording studio, and my busy performing schedule. I'm also under contract to perform with him whenever he's hired to do a live gig. Work with my jobbing orchestra picked up in the spring but waned throughout the summer, when the bandleader planned to record a new CD and then hit the road to promote it. Sadly that didn't come together, so I had

MY FUTURE ROCK AND ROLLERS, HANNAH AND GRAHAM.

to pick up whatever subbing gigs I could find. Some of the seeds I sowed last winter for Maryann and The Professors came to fruition with gigs during the summer months. One of the country clubs that received our band's promo kit hired us to play their annual rock-and-roll night. Private events included summer parties at various suburban homes, one at a country club, and a surprise sixtieth birthday party. We played half a dozen bar gigs, something we hadn't done in at least five years. We also performed several outdoor lunch concerts at downtown office buildings, plus four summer concert nights for different suburban park districts. The wedding ad from Craig's List that I responded to on Day 17 ended up hiring us to play their reception – a great dividend from the 30 second investment! We were very proud to be selected as one of 12 musical acts out of hundreds who applied to be showcased performers at the 2008 SPRA conference.

We're very happy with our new keyboard player. He plays every gig with us, whether club date, festival, wedding, or private party. Our original keyboardist joins us for the private-sector work. When he does, we're an incredibly tight six-piece unit. Our bass player situation worked out a bit differently. The fellow we hired to replace our departed bassist played a club date and one summer concert with us. The new bass player had eight weeks to learn our repertoire, and he managed to master only the club-type music we play. As a result, we asked our former bass player to perform at the private parties, which involves an entirely different selection of songs. The new bass player was aware of this, understanding that we had to do what was necessary to make sure these gigs came off without a hitch, especially since private parties are where we make the real money. We had so much fun being reunited with our old bass player that I literally threw myself at his feet and begged him to come back. He admitted that he missed playing with us, and his replacement agreed it made sense to switch back since he knew all the material and was capable of providing far more in the way of vocals. Everyone is ecstatic that he's returned.